POWER RECOVERY

THE TWELVE STEPS FOR A NEW GENERATION

JAMES WILEY

PAULIST PRESS
New York and Mahwah, N.J.

MONKS OF MT. TABOR

Cover Design by James F. Brisson, Williamsville, VT.

Library of Congress Cataloging-in-Publication Data

Wiley, James, 1920-
    Power recovery : the twelve steps for a new generation / by James Wiley.
        p.   cm.
    ISBN 0-8091-3552-3
    1. Alcoholics—Rehabilitation. 2. Alcoholics—Rehabilitation—Case studies. 3. Narcotic addicts—Rehabilitation. 4. Alcoholics Anonymous. 5. Twelve-step programs. I. Title.
HV5275.W55   1995   94-43302
616.86′106—dc20   CIP

Published by Paulist Press
997 Macarthur Boulevard
Mahwah, NJ 07430

Printed and bound in the
United States of America

THE ORIGINAL TWELVE STEPS
OF ALCOHOLICS ANONYMOUS

1. We admitted we were powerless over alcohol—that our lives had become unmanageable.
2. Came to believe that a Power greater than ourselves could restore us to sanity.
3. Made a decision to turn our will and our lives over to the care of God *as we understood Him.*
4. Made a searching and fearless moral inventory of ourselves.
5. Admitted to God, to ourselves, and to another human being the exact nature of our wrongs.
6. Were entirely ready to have God remove all these defects of character.
7. Humbly asked Him to remove our shortcomings.
8. Made a list of all persons we had harmed, and became willing to make amends to them all.
9. Made direct amends to such people wherever possible, except when to do so would injure them or others.
10. Continued to take personal inventory and when we were wrong promptly admitted it.
11. Sought through prayer and meditation to improve our conscious contact with God *as we understood Him,* praying only for knowledge of His will for us and the power to carry that out.
12. Having had a spiritual awakening as the result of these steps, we tried to carry this message to alcoholics, and to practice these principles in all our affairs.

ACKNOWLEDGEMENTS

My thanks to Bill W. and Dr. Bob, the co-founders of A. A., for getting it started in the first place and blazing the trail. I am grateful to the members of my A. A. group, who shared their stories with me and encouraged me to write the book. I value the friendship of my editor, Richard Sparks, whose patience and suggestions helped shape the book. To my sponsor, Arthur R., who opened the door for me—my love and heartfelt thanks. Most of all, I thank my Higher Power for being there for me when the door was opened, and for being my partner in this effort.

My love and my gratitude go to my wife, Margaret, for her wisdom and her support. To the many young people, and the older ones, too, who opened their hearts and shared their experiences in these pages, my indebtedness and my admiration know no bounds. I salute them for carrying the message in the great tradition.

CONTENTS

PART ONE: HOOK IN, POWER UP AND GET WELL

PART TWO: A TWELVE STEPS WORKSHOP

PROLOGUE: SYLVIA

In my freshman year in high school, the day of Christmas break, I got arrested. I was smoking pot in the girls' bathroom at school when a teacher walked in. They searched me. I had pills of all kinds in my purse. They handcuffed me and, in front of the entire student body, they walked me to where my mother was standing beside the police car, crying. I got in the car and they took me away. I was fourteen.

My name is Sylvia. I am an alcoholic and an addict, sober six years.

I didn't like reality. I was always trying to live in a fantasy world, making up dreams for the future about what I was going to do, and who I was going to be, about how elegant and sophisticated I would become. I would dream these dreams while I had a dollar bill stuck up my nose and my face pressed against a glass with cocaine on it.

Yet I was raised by my mother to be a good church girl, to have nice clothes, to speak well, to dress well, and to present myself like a lady. My parents were divorced when I was three, and my father moved out. I grew up with my mother and my sister, who is also an alcoholic and an addict.

My parents pitted us against one another, using the children as a power play, and always trying to hurt the other through the children. It was always kind of a mind game, about taking sides. I was raised, I think, to hate my father. From the time I was born and through the divorce, my mother was dating the doctor she worked for. He was the only father figure I knew. When I was twelve, I find out, "Oh, my God, this man is married, and has been married all this time, and I was lied to."

The first time that I ever drank to get drunk, I blacked out, passed out and threw up for four hours. And that became my pattern. I came into public school when I was about eleven, and at school I felt very inadequate. I didn't fit in and I wasn't accepted.

My schoolmates were drinking, so I started drinking, stealing alcohol from the liquor cabinet and bringing it to school. And all of a sudden I started to fit in somewhere. By the time I got to high school I knew how to do drugs. I knew what they were, I knew how to get them and where to get them. I went to church a lot because my drug dealer went to the same church, so I was happy to go.

When I got back to school two weeks after being arrested at Christmas break, I had gone from using drugs and alcohol once a week to doing it three and four times every day. Over Christmas break, I became very popular. Everybody knew who I was. People thought I had status: I had been cuffed and taken downtown. Suddenly I had lots of friends.

In school I was hanging out with people who stole cars, dealt drugs and hurt people. We would start drinking and smoking at six-thirty in the morning and by eight-thirty we would be at school. We'd go back out at lunch time, party after school and party at night. On the weekends we did our real serious stuff. That's when we got into the cocaine, the speed and the harder drugs.

My sister and I got caught with drugs. My mother found the cocaine and some rolling papers in our room. My parents took us to a counselor who said we belonged in an in-patient treatment center. The next thing we knew we were in the car and on the way to the hospital. We still had all our drugs with us.

All my life I had felt crazy, as though there was something wrong with me. The only time I felt somewhat normal was when I had my drugs and my alcohol. And now they were taking it away from me, and these people were going to find out I was really crazy. I was dragged, kicking, screaming and fighting into this treatment center.

I was fifteen when I got out of treatment. They told me in A. A., "You have to change your playmates and your playthings." But my terminal uniqueness kicked in, and I said, "No, not me." So I went out with the same friends and we went to the same places. The man that I was in love with had been a high school drop-out, the drug dealer, and when I got sober he decided that he wanted to get sober.

This was not in my game plan. I wasn't serious about it; I was just kind of playing along. But he got serious. He would go to A. A. meetings, and he would listen, and he would share, and he had a sponsor. I felt, "O my God, my life is truly over; they've got him, too."

I continued going to meetings. I stayed in the program and I stayed sober. And I had begun to hear things in the meetings that started to make a little bit of sense, things that were making me feel I wasn't quite so crazy.

My problem was that I continued to be with the same people. I couldn't let go of the past. It's as though you're in a whirlwind, and all of a sudden you have to stop it and whirl in a different direction.

I see young people today in the program stuck in that whirlwind, but they've still got their hand out and they're still holding on to those old playmates—and doing the same things that they used to do.

And that's exactly what I did. I wouldn't let go. And I picked up that drink. I got drunk. But something had changed. I still wasn't really excited about sobriety, but I felt guilty, ashamed. I felt I had lost something.

So I went back to A. A. and I started listening. I went to lots of meetings. And I got a sponsor. And I called her. I started working the Twelve Steps.

But I was terrified to be happy. Because when I finally started to work the steps and miracles started coming true in my life, I was very stand-offish from the joy and excitement that came with all that. I thought, "Sylvia, this is serious stuff. It is not a game. If

I enjoy it too much, if I'm too happy about it, then it might be taken away from me." So I held off as long as I could.

I finally broke one day, and I said, "I have got to have fun! I am dying here!" Now, today, people think I am some kind of a nut case because I am always bouncing off walls, hopping around making very little sense, having so much fun.

I still hear young people in meetings say in this mournful voice things like, "I am so grateful to be sober; thank you for my sobriety," and there is no joy in their voices. I want to shake them. Because the Big Book tells us, "We aren't a glum lot. We absolutely insist on enjoying life."

I think it's great to smile, to be happy and laugh—and not at the expense of others. Today my joy does not come from that. Today I can laugh at myself and laugh with other people.

My God says today, "Sylvia, enjoy the world. I give you trees, I give you birds, I give you animals and flowers, and then I give you the people that surround you." Who am I to say, "No, thank you. This is serious business. I can't enjoy those things."

That's what they are there for. That's why I'm here, and that's why I'm sober today. And I have another chance at life.

Sylvia T. is one of 148 young recovered alcoholics and addicts who tell portions of their experiences in these pages. Each has a prologue to recovery. While their stories are different, in most of them there are striking similarities to Sylvia's problems with family, alcohol and drugs.

PART ONE

Hook In, Power Up and Get Well

"You may be limping along with only ten watts of power, because that's all you dialed in, when actually 250,000 watts are available to you. You have to claim the power."—Brian N.

INTRODUCTION

"The first time I read the Big Book, ALCOHOLICS ANONY-MOUS, I thought it was quaint," said Susan L. in an A. A. meeting. "It was written in 1939, twenty-six years before I was born, and the language, the people and the customs of the 1930s seemed archaic, like something from another time warp."

"Whoa! Don't knock the Big Book!" was my defensive reaction to Susan's remark. ALCOHOLICS ANONYMOUS, A. A.'s Big Book, is the standard work on the Twelve Step program of recovery from alcoholism. But I knew, as Susan did, that for more than half a century, since its publication in 1939, the basic text of the book has remained unchanged, never updated through three editions and forty-nine printings.

"Could there really be," I wondered later, "a three-generation communications gap between young alcoholics and addicts of today and the 1939 prose of the Big Book? Are their experiences today really so different?"

"Check it out," I said to myself. So for two years I sat on a metal chair with a small notebook and chronicled the confusion, the fear and the pain, as well as the insights, the breakthroughs and the humor shared by young recovering alcoholics and addicts in more than 400 A. A. meetings.

Susan was not alone in her discomfort. I heard other comments.

"I was reading the Big Book the other day," said Jessie T., "and I thought, 'When is this thing going to talk to me?'"

"It took me several years to read the Big Book and understand it," said Leslie D.

Then Tony C. spoke out in a beginners' meeting: "I know how

to work a computer, a drill press, and how to work on my car," said Tony, "but I don't know how to work a step, like in the Twelve Steps. I've read the Big Book, but I can't find the instructions. Tell me, just how do you *work* a *step*?"

I found that, to a generation which grew up on TV, video games and computer monitors, the Big Book often does represent a challenge. Yet despite grumbling, some were reading the book. Some were getting the message verbally from sponsors or by talking and sharing among themselves. "We don't know how to work the steps," said Grita W. "We learn to work them by learning from others how they learned to work them."

In the meetings, they spoke of their despair as they cratered out. They told of their fumbles as they tried to work the steps to get clean and sober and straighten out their lives. I discovered that while the fundamental nature of the alcoholic personality is not much changed since 1939, the packaging, the scenarios, the lifestyles, the language idioms and the belief systems have changed radically. Attitudes toward sex, relationships, marriage, family, career, and money are significantly different. A major difference is the acceptance of the reality of widespread dual addiction. The alcoholic and the drug addict are often one and the same.[1]

I learned that today, alcoholics and addicts start earlier and crash and burn sooner. Most start drinking and using drugs at twelve and thirteen. In Alcoholics Anonymous, one-quarter of all A. A.s are under thirty and more than half the members worldwide are under forty. In Narcotics Anonymous, forty-eight percent of its members are under thirty, and another forty-eight percent are between thirty and forty-five. Over forty-five?

"There are no old addicts," said one junkie.

---

[1] "Can a pill or drug taker, who also has a genuine alcoholic history, become a member of A. A.? Yes "—Bill W., cofounder of A. A., *The Grapevine*

As I listened, I became aware that the word *power* is very much a part of young people's vocabulary. I began hearing talk of power: "I felt my power...." "She took my power . " "I had the power to...."

"At thirty days' sobriety I had no power in my life," said Susie N. "And the one thing I wanted was power over the things in my life. But now my Higher Power has given me power to have things in my life again."

As alcoholics and addicts, we lost our power to our addictions—they had power over us. In recovery, we begin to realize that our power loss is profound. We have lost self-esteem, jobs, lovers or spouses, even the roofs over our heads. Admitting that we are powerless hits us where we live.

I remembered that recovery means finding again something that is lost. As we get clean and sober, we become concerned with recovering our power: physical, mental, emotional, financial, sexual. Then we see others around us finding their power through a process of spiritual discovery or spiritual renewal, and we decide to try it for ourselves.

In another meeting, one remark snapped it all together and summed up in simple language the power which so many of us find in the Twelve Steps.

"I learned how to stop drinking and drugging during the first thirty days of treatment," said Ross N. "But if that is all you do, you go crazy! Working the Twelve Steps is what made me sane, happy and free, and what gave me back my power. When I hang out with my Higher Power, I get the power to make the changes I need to make in my life."

Those two years of listening have triggered a book about young people and power—about abusing it, losing it and getting it back again. It is a book about sharing: sharing what it is like to be scared, confused, hurting and addicted to alcohol and drugs. It is about finding a way out. The book takes a new look at the Twelve Steps of recovery through the eyes and experiences of contemporary people who are living clean, sober, successful lives right now.

It is intended as a youthful running mate to the Big Book. The role of this work is that of a facilitator speaking in many voices, bridging from the classic precepts of the Big Book to the velocity of lifestyles circa 2000.

The facilitators are one hundred and forty-eight young recovered alcoholics and drug addicts who openly share their discoveries, their thoughts and their feelings with you in these pages.

It is both a how-to book and a peer group counseling guide. The text is a continuing dialogue between the author, explaining traditional Twelve Step therapy, and the young people who interject their own comments on how it was with them as they came unglued, hit bottom, came into recovery, and learned how to turn their lives around. Together we tackle a big stumbling block to sobriety—the fact that alcoholics and substance abusers are often quite hostile toward any discussion of spiritual values.

"When they first mentioned God to me in these meetings, I wanted to rip their faces off," said Eric L.

We show how we learned to find our own concept of a power greater than ourselves, learned how to hook into that power, receive spiritual sustenance, and claim our own personal empowerment. This is the theme of the book: the premise that there exists somewhere in this universe a supernatural Energy, a Force that likes us, a Power that can be accessed by us to help us. How to connect with that power is the message of this book.

The book proposes a structured method of working the Twelve Steps for those who are comfortable with such an approach. The recommended way to use the book is to first read in Part One a chapter on a step, then turn to Part Two for the Work Plan for that step. Each Work Plan offers study assignments and writing exercises and gives easy-to-follow instructions designed to help readers get their individual input into working each step.

In this book, those stories of a personal and confidential nature were voluntarily shared by young A. A. members who came to my home, told their stories into my tape recorder, and gave me permission to use them. Other stories are from talks given by anonymous speakers at open A. A. meetings where talks were taped, and tapes were made available. All such stories are printed with permission of the speakers, provided their anonymity is respected. To this purpose, all names and locales have been changed. Briefer comments were jotted down in discussion meetings of my home group with the consent of members of the group. They knew I was writing a book about young recovering alcoholics, they trusted me, and put up with my scribbling.

"When I'm speaking, and Jim takes out his notebook and starts writing, I feel I must be growing in my program!" Mike T. told the group.

The point of the book is this: that so many young people, addicted, undisciplined and unbelieving, have found a faith in a power greater than themselves, a faith that enabled them to make remarkable changes in their lives. They have done it with grace and humor. It is very much their book.

In our conversations together in these pages, we have tried to present the Twelve Steps as the exciting journey which we found them to be.

"Early in my sobriety," recalled Steve D., "a guy said to me, 'If you get sober, fasten your seat belt, man. It's a ride!'"

Chapter One

CRASHING AND BURNING

"When the stuff stops working but you can't stop drinking and can't stop drugging, then you have got a real control problem."—Ted S.

First Step: We admitted we were powerless over alcohol and drugs—that our lives had become unmanageable.

"From fourteen to twenty-six, I was in six treatment centers and five detox units," said Teresa T. "And finally one day something deep inside me said, 'The war is over, Teresa—give up.' It was total surrender. That was when I finally started getting well."

The First Step is like running out of gas a million miles from nowhere. You try to start the engine, then even the battery goes dead. You are totally without power. That's how the First Step feels in the beginning. And yet the curious paradox is that this is also the step where we start getting our power back. But before we can do that, we have to admit we are powerless over alcohol and drugs, and that our lives have become unmanageable.

"I lost it," people sometimes say when they mess up. As alcoholics and addicts, we messed up. Drinking alcohol, smoking dope, sniffing white powder, shooting up, we lost it. We cratered out. Getting our power back is hard work. The First Step is where we begin to find it again.

The purpose of Step One is to help you to stop drinking and stop using drugs, and to show you how to stay stopped—that is square one and bottom line. The step aims to open our eyes so that we can see for ourselves that we suffer from a progressive disease that can kill us. It helps us to see that our recovery won't last unless we first admit total defeat, and that we don't have to do it alone—we are in this together.

WHO WE ARE

Like Teresa, who opens this chapter, we recovered alcoholics and addicts who speak to you in this book have each had our moment of truth when we had to admit we were powerless over alcohol and drugs, and were slowly destroying ourselves. On top of that, we have a lot more in common. Most of us are in our twenties, though some are younger and a few are older. As kids, the majority of us felt different and felt we didn't fit in. Nearly all of us started drinking and using drugs at eleven or twelve.

"The first time I got drunk I was twelve," said Gary D. "It was with two other guys. We had a bottle of Bacardi rum and a bottle of vodka. I downed most of the Bacardi. I made it to my bed and I didn't throw up. That's all I remember. Later, my friend told me I had run around naked in a shopping center and pissed on all the shop windows. I thought, 'If I can do that, I can do anything.'"

Multiple Addictions

"By the time I was thirteen, I was doing drugs and alcohol all the time—I mean every day," said Juan F.

The reality is that many of us had at least two and possibly several addictions to various chemical substances. There may have been one favorite drug of choice, but alcohol was the common denominator with all of them.

"When we look at our various addictions, it's like looking out into the same yard from different windows," said Lisa M.

Virtually all of us were in denial about our alcoholism and addictions.

"My denial rejected the fact that I was an alcoholic," said Molly N. "Crazy was more acceptable."

"I was in such denial I could be kneeling in the street, bleed-

MONKS OF MT. TABOR

ing, puking and crying," said Alan G., "and some kind stranger might walk up to me and say, 'May I help you?' and I would say, 'No, thanks, I can handle it.'"

Relationship Problems

"Going into an Alcoholics Anonymous meeting and asking about relationships is like going into the paraplegics' ward and asking how to run the fastest mile," said Lynn C. "They've been through five or six marriages and *they're* telling *you* how to do life?"

Alcoholics and addicts have terrible relationship problems. These are probably the second greatest cause of slips and relapses —the first is complacency. Often the pain that results when a relationship is breaking up is the final trigger that causes us to hit bottom in the first place and seek help.

"To eliminate the pain," said Gregory G., "we go from one relationship right into another. And you give that person the power to hurt you. You are not ready to go through that hurt again."

A Dysfunctional Generation

"I am not a skid-row bum," said Brian S. "I grew up in an upper middle class family where both my parents were alcoholics, but where their image was important to them. I had a lot of that in me, too."

For the most part, our families are dysfunctional. As in Brian's case, we are apt to be second generation or third generation alcoholics and addicts. Often our parents were divorced. We were swapped back and forth between mothers and fathers. We shared homes with one or several step-parents or live-in lovers of mom or dad. Not infrequently we were abused—verbally, emotionally, physically or sexually. Some of us are incest survivors.

"Most of us don't know what a functional family is," said Scott H. "Dysfunctional is normal. This is a dysfunctional generation."

WHERE WE ARE COMING FROM

"At my second A. A. meeting," said Dyana Y., "I showed up dressed just right, looking real good. A lady sitting next to me leaned over and whispered, 'You look so absolutely terrific outside, you must be a mess inside.' But she said it kindly. She knew where I was coming from. I broke down and started crying."

Some of us, like Dyana, showed up looking great. We gave the impression we had it all together when we were actually coming unglued. Yet others came into recovery cold turkey, looking awful, feeling sick, depressed, even suicidal. We were running on empty.

Still others made it into recovery via the treatment center route.

"I loved my treatment center. I went back six times," said Lynn C. "Every morning they gave me my big fix of Thioridazine to make me feel good, and they kept telling me, 'Dear, it's all your mother's fault.'"

Being Scared and Defiant

"I was scared," said Rolando J. "I saw those tacky bumper-sticker slogans and those twelve religious-sounding rules tacked up on the wall. I said, 'What am I doing here? This is unreal.' Then this big biker type came up to me—long hair, metal-studded leather vest, big muscles—and said to me, 'Man, if you want what I got, you are in the right place.' I panicked. I said, 'I'm out of here!' and I was. Ten months later I hit bottom and was back."

You may feel reluctant, scared and defiant when you come into recovery. Nobody really wants to be there in the beginning.

"I was twenty years old when I came to my first A. A. meeting, and I thought, 'It's over—my life is over,'" said Terry F. "Everybody was about forty, and that's when you're supposed to start dying. Somehow I didn't see the young people around my own age."

It is okay to be scared. It is okay to be defiant. Quite a few of us were that way at the start. But we soon found that Alcoholics Anonymous is the lifeline we had been looking for. Yet the real deal, we discovered, is that the Twelve Step program is a formula for a great new way of living our lives.

ADMITTING WE ARE POWERLESS

"I was addicted to alcohol, to drugs, to sex, and to food," said Carol L. "I was bulimic and anorexic. I was powerless over everything. But in the program, I learned that what I was really addicted to was escape. What form it took didn't matter."

Admitting we are powerless is the key that starts up our recovery.

Powerless means simply without power—we had no power to stop drinking alcohol, using drugs and doing our other addictions. Like Teresa and Carol, we need to honestly admit this to ourselves. And then we need to admit it out loud to our sponsors and to members of our home group. Only then can we move on to our personal miracles of recovery.

The Pain in Step One

"We had to keep drinking and drugging," said Molly N., "because when you took away the anesthetic, the pain became unbearable."

There is a lot of pain in the First Step. It hurts to feel so hopeless and helpless, and not know what to do. It hurts to admit that your alcoholism and your addictions have you completely licked.

"I want to design my own reality, and it would be pain-free," said Ross N. "But that is not reality."

Part of the pain is grief—grieving for what was, grieving for the times when everything was good, grieving for the old self in us that is dying when the new self has not yet emerged.

"Pain is part of being young," said Tracy T. "I had to accept that I am going to be uncomfortable for a while."

Powerless But Not Helpless

"I am powerless over alcohol and drugs, but I am not helpless," said Hal N.

Remember that it says we are powerless over alcohol and drugs, not powerless over everything in our lives. We can apply this powerless-but-not-helpless attitude to our problems of daily living. Here is an exercise which you can use to make that belief become real in your program. Say to yourself:

I am powerless over chemicals, but I am not helpless because I can

1. Go to a meeting.
2. Speak up in the meeting and share my problems with the group.
3. Meet and talk with my sponsor.
4. Live one day at a time.
5. Read the Big Book.
6. Refuse to isolate myself. Get with people instead.
7. Stay away from bars and drug scenes.
8. Telephone a friend in the program.
9. Be a participant, not just an observer, in meetings.
10. Stay away from a drink or a drug one day at a time.

Think, then write your own list of ten other ways in which you are not helpless. The objective is to show you the many options you actually have.

"In the First Step I realized, 'This is not just treatment, meetings and recovery,'" said Chris P. "I thought, 'This is the next stage of my life. I am already in it. I am right where I am supposed to be.'"

Admitting, Accepting and Surrendering

After a while, we come to understand the first part of Step One at three different levels. First, we admit we are powerless over alcohol and drugs. But we can admit it and still feel rebellious, resentful and trapped—right? Later, there comes acceptance. We admit and accept our addictions. However, we can accept something and still feel sad, deprived and cheated. The final level of understanding comes when we completely surrender to the knowledge that we are indeed an alcoholic and an addict, and are at peace with it. Until we reach surrender, the struggle is still going on in us.

"Surrender means 'Give up—just plain flat give up,'" said Rob S.

With surrender usually comes serenity. No longer do we question, "Am I really an alcoholic? Am I really an addict?" We know.

OUR UNMANAGEABLE LIVES

"During the last year of my drinking, I had been fired from my job, kicked out by my parents, and dumped by my girl friend," said Dick E. "I couldn't pay the rent on my apartment, so I was living out of my car. But I couldn't understand that my life was unmanageable."

Sometimes it is hard to understand how out of control our own lives really were. Wrecked cars, D.W.I. tickets, getting put in jail, beating up on a girl friend, trashing a bar, losing jobs—these seemed just a run of bad luck. Sonja L. couldn't get a handle on it either. "At first I could not get the second half of the step," Sonja said. "Then one day I substituted the word 'unbearable' for 'unmanageable.' That I could understand. I got through the step this way until I finally was able to realize how crazy my life had been."

We had problems because we created the problems. In Step One, by seeing how we messed up, we begin to stop creating problems for ourselves.

Learning Humility

"The back seat of a police car is a great breeding ground for humility," said Greg M.

In this step, we begin to understand true humility, which is the quality of becoming humble and teachable. Yet even when hand-cuffed, we alcoholics and addicts sometimes fail to get the message about humility.

We may think humility means having been put down, made to feel less than others, or getting caught doing something bad. Yes, it can mean these things, yet three of the dictionary meanings of humility are *kindness, courtesy* and *deference*. That may make humility seem a little less distasteful. The Twelve Step program recommends that we go through an ego deflation adjustment. What it means is that we had to come to grips with our conceited-ness, our pride and our arrogance. We needed to look at the feeling within us that made us think we were better and smarter than others. Our egos got us into trouble. We were trapped in our egos, and this distorted our perceptions. We got locked up in our unmanageable way of life.

"Alcoholism is the only prison where the locks are on the inside," said Deanna L. "The program gives me twelve keys to get out of that prison."

THE POWER IN THE FIRST STEP

When we first come in, when we make the decision to stop drinking and using, even as we admit our very powerlessness, a power begins to work in us though we may not be aware of it.

The First Power

"The first power that comes is the power not to pick up a drink or a drug when everything in you tells you to do it," said Lisa M. "You get the power to put it off one hour at a time, one day at a time."

This is the power that switches on as a result of going to lots of meetings, not drinking or using between meetings, getting a sponsor, using that sponsor, and getting into the steps. It is the feeling of physical and mental well-being that comes as our bodies and our minds respond to no longer being used as chemical dumps.

"I feel such a power in not drinking," said Gloria Y., celebrating thirty days of sobriety. "I feel as if I have discovered a secret power."

"Going to a meeting is like going to an orgy," said Katie N. "You come out feeling better, and you're not quite sure who is responsible for it."

The Power in "We"

"The purpose of Step One is to find you," said Richard L., "and we can help you find you."

It is no accident that "we" is the first word in the First Step. "We" is implied in every one of the Twelve Steps. This one word sums up the working philosophy of the steps. Together we admit that by ourselves we can no longer cope. Together we admit we need help. Together we ask for help. Together we find our strength and our power in the "we-ness" of the program. The We Power comes when we start speaking up in meetings and sharing our experiences and our feelings with others. It does not come if we remain a spectator, sitting in the back row near the door. We must be a participant in the interaction of the group if we are to get well.

Little by little, we learn to trust again. The experience of bonding with a group of fellow human beings is what some of us have yearned for. For some, it may be the first time it has ever happened—to be accepted unconditionally and welcomed just as we are. When this happens, we get the feeling that we fit, we belong, and that we are truly a part of the group.

Jump-Starting Your Power

In the meantime, here are seven areas in which you can begin to jump-start some power in your life. Realize that there is power available to you in:

1. Choices—the power to make right choices.
2. Hope—the power to expect your own good.
3. Gratitude—the power to be truly thankful.
4. The group—your power support system.
5. The slogans—powerful wisdom handed down.
6. Your sponsor—the power of a good teacher.
7. Becoming spiritually open—the real source of power.

Gradually we start to get our power back and find people we can trust. "I told my sponsor the other day that after two years I finally trusted him," said Dan Y. "He led me to a mirror and told me to look in. 'No,' he said, 'you finally trust yourself. You can now say "Yes, Sir!" to yourself.'"

BEING OPEN TO CHANGE

"Alcoholics and addicts get in a rut, and they stay there," said Toni G. "They like it there. Give an alcoholic a rut and he'll move in and furnish it."

We feel safe in our ruts because we don't like change. But to get well, we have to open ourselves up to change. The point is to leave one place and move on to another. So the following workouts may help you to get moving.

Six Ways To Begin To Change

The take-home message of the First Step is this: change, or die. We need to change our thinking and our behavior. Strange, but it often works better if we change the actions first and let the changes in thinking follow.

Try this: Each morning, ask yourself: "With me, is it that I cannot change—or *will not change*?" Then take some action in one of these areas:

1. Begin to change awareness—we see but do not perceive.
2. Begin to change your actions.
3. Begin to change your attitudes.

4. Change your playmates, your old buddies.
5. Change your playpens, your old hang-outs.
6. Change your patterns: Call your sponsor, go to a meeting.

"I can't do change in quantum leaps," said Carlos M. "I have to do it in little baby steps. If you can't do big change, just rearrange things a little."

Replaying Your Life Videotape

To help you begin to change in the First Step, you need to see and understand more clearly your own powerlessness and how your life became unmanageable. How do you do this? Since we alcoholics and addicts are good at fantasy trips, you might try this fantasizing exercise. Visualize yourself rewinding a videotape of your life from the present moment back to the time when you first started drinking and drugging. Then run the tape forward, hitting the pause button from time to time as you watch your own soap opera unfold on the screen. Watch yourself, time after time, giving your power away to alcohol, drugs, other people and situations. Study all your big scenes each time you were out of control or messed up.

Writing your own critic's review of your performance will take you deep into working the First Step. The Work Plan for Step One in Part Two of this book offers more exercises for getting in touch with your powerlessness and the ways in which your life became unmanageable.

"Alcoholics don't believe in themselves," said Hal N. "They think that if they start doing these Twelve Steps, nothing will happen inside them. They don't realize that in the actual doing of it, they will change."

Chapter Two

BEGINNING TO HEAL

*"I was totally out of touch with sanity.
My sponsor told me, 'You have two 747s
flying around in your head and radar can
pick up only one.'"*–Karl C.

Second Step: Came to believe that a power greater than ourselves could restore us to sanity.

"The transition from the First Step into the Second Step is like jumping out of an airplane without a parachute," said Randy B. in a step study meeting. "Powerless and really terrified, the alcoholic plunges down, seeing the earth rushing up at him. Then, just ten feet before impact, a hidden hand reaches out and grabs him, and a small voice says, 'Excuse me, we're conducting a survey—do you believe in God?'"

Step Two is centered on the inner battle that goes on inside many alcoholics and addicts: "Could there really be a Higher Power who cares about me?"

The Second Step helps us to resolve this question. Up front, we need to look at the resistance we may feel about this step, because most chemically dependent people have a spiritual problem as well as an addiction problem. Through neglect or outright rejection, we may have steered away from anything that smacked of spiritual values. What's more, lots of us have a problem with authority figures and, to us, God represented the ultimate put-down authority figure.

The Debate

In the Second Step, we may feel shoved toward a spiritual encounter we would rather sidestep. The idea may make us uncomfortable, even angry. Here are some current viewpoints. Can you identify with these feelings?

"First you make me admit defeat, then you hit me with this God stuff when I am down. Back off!" said Mikey P.

"Going into the Second Step, I said to God, 'I don't want to be intimate with you. You will ask of me what I can't deliver,'" said Vicki C.

"God? I dumped him years ago," said Debbie G.

"I can swallow everything about the program except the God thing," said Walter T.

"We don't like that 'G' word," said Wayne T.

"I didn't need a Higher Power," said Jeanne A. "I was my own Higher Power."

"I thought God was going to fry my ass because I liked girls and whisky," said Diego R.

If you find yourself relating to these comments, keep in mind that it does not have to mean God in the old-fashioned, strict, forbidding sense when it says "a power greater than ourselves"—the concept is much wider. And "restore us to sanity" does not mean you were a candidate for an asylum. You can be sure, too, that nobody is going to give you orders and tell you what you must do. Remember also that we are all different. Some of us had very strict religious backgrounds. Some of us had none at all.

"In the first six months of my sobriety, I had not come to believe in anything," said Brent L. "My attitude then was, 'I don't trust you, I don't trust myself, and I certainly don't trust God.'"

To many of us, the idea that there might be a Higher Power who was interested in our case seemed too remote, too childish, and even a little threatening. We argued the matter with our sponsors.

"You want to get into a debate about religion," said Randy B., "and your sponsor may point out that you just recently took off the plastic wrist band from a nut ward."

A POWER GREATER THAN OURSELVES

"We are pretty desperate when we come in," said Frank Y., "and faith often has its beginning in desperation. When we discover that our Higher Power is trustworthy in some big deal, we begin to trust it more in little things as well."

A power greater than yourself may have already touched your life in ways you hadn't recognized. Try this exercise: In one corner of your mind, create an imaginary file directory just as you would create a directory in a computer. Title the directory "Higher Power Action." Then open a series of files under that directory. Put names on the files such as:

1. The time Higher Power saved me when ...
2. The time Higher Power arranged money for me when ...
3. The time Higher Power got me out of trouble when ...

Make up your own file names as you recall incidents when some force beyond yourself—coincidence maybe?—came to your rescue.

"To me, the beginning of my faith was deciding that there were no coincidences," said Charmaine E.

Getting It on Our Own Terms

The Big Book gives us the key to Step Two right off the bat, on page 12, when it throws down the challenge: *"Why don't you choose your own conception of God?"* It even prints it in italics like that, for emphasis. It backs up the message on page 46: "We did not need to consider another's conception of God. Our own conception, however inadequate, was sufficient to make the approach and to effect a contact with Him."

While many of us are cynical toward religion, others are hungry for some form of spiritual nurturing that makes sense to us. We became spiritual comparison shoppers, checking out eastern religions and New Age movements.

"I had looked all over for that Higher Power," said Ronnie P. "I went to a bunch of churches of every denomination, you name it. I couldn't find it. But the Second Step taught me that this Higher Power is inside me."

What we seek is a spiritual concept that will fit our own needs, one that has room for our own ideas of what a Higher Power is—or isn't. We want a jeans and T-shirt approach to spirituality that involves lots of loving and caring, with a support group of our like-minded peers. Ironically, while A. A. is the last place most of us thought to look for it, we are discovering our spirituality in the Twelve Step program. We find our spiritual support systems in the huggy-touchy camaraderie of the fellowship.

"In A. A., God has evolved into a generic God—a God who is acceptable to anyone of any faith," said Dennis Y.

COMING TO BELIEVE

The Second Step comes to some of us with complete ease. It slips over us like an old familiar garment. It came to André T. this way:

"I started to feel very good, very loved inside. The healing began right away with me because I opened myself up to this love, to the Higher Power. At about three months of sobriety, I had gone out with some friends in the program. I came home that night, and for the first time in my life I had this enormous feeling that there was a God, and that he did love me. It was so real, the experience overwhelmed me.

"I used to describe in meetings that it was better than any drug I had ever done, better than any high that I had ever experienced. Because it was real, and it was the love of God. I'll never forget that."

A Concept with Lots of Room

Unlike André, others of us approach the Second Step more cautiously, and we need more time to sniff around it and examine it. When we look at it, we realize that the core of the step is a belief system—the expectation that there exists somewhere in this universe some kind of mystical power which has the power to unscramble our mixed-up thinking and get us back on track.

"My sponsor used to say to me, 'Did the sun go down last night?'" said Tom L. "I would say, 'Yes.' Next he would ask, 'Did it come up this morning?' and I would answer, 'Yes.' Then he would ask, 'Did you have anything to do with it?' and I would say, 'No.' And then he would say, 'So there is a power greater than ourselves, don't you think?' And I would have to answer, 'Yes.'"

The step reads, "came to believe *that*," not "believe *in*." So if you have reservations, all you have to do is believe *that* it is possible some such power could exist. Some are not comfortable with a power that is cast in a male image, and prefer to speak of a Higher Power as she, her, or it—and go with that concept. It works.

"It bothers me to have the masculine or the feminine pronouns for God," said Opal M. "I feel that God is not a him or a her. I believe that it is a Higher Power that we can't define. For myself, if I define it as a him or her, then I bring it human qualities. I don't think the Higher Power has anything to do with our humanness—it's not on the same plane as we are."

"I don't see God as being masculine or feminine," said Leonora P. "Him bothers me more than her, because when I grew up Catholic, I saw men sitting on the throne. I find it liberating when the female pronoun is used. We're in such a bind in our language that we have to go one way or the other."

"He really doesn't care what you call him as long as you stay in touch," said Keith F.

The Real Secret

"Coming to believe is a process," said Ken M. "Resist it, and it doesn't work. Work it furiously, and it doesn't work. But lean into it and let it flow over you, and it usually works."

What Ken said is really the big secret of coming to believe: Let it happen, and let it happen at its own pace. That is essentially what we are talking about in Step Two: leaning into it and letting it flow over you.

There is really no mystery to coming to believe. This is the way you come to believe anything. It is very simple: You hang out with people you know and like, you talk with them and listen to what they believe, and pretty soon you come to believe it, too. In coming to believe, you just let it happen—but when it finally does happen for you, then it is like a leap of the human spirit toward the mystical Spirit, and an embrace between the two.

The Group as Higher Power

"I want to thank the group for my Higher Power," said Marilyn G. as she celebrated her sixth month of sobriety. "Every day I hear him in your voices. And every day I see him in your eyes."

"If you have trouble thinking God, think Higher Power, think Energy," said Becky N. "When you walk into a meeting and you feel the energy in that room, you know your Higher Power is there in the group. When you feel that energy in a person, you know your Higher Power is there, too."

When we identify with a group and begin to feel we are a part of it, many of us come to look upon the group as our first Higher Power. So it is a good idea to attach yourself to a home group. Go to every meeting they have. As we go regularly to the same group, a bonding begins to take place.

"I remember the first meeting at which I suddenly felt connected at the navel with everybody in the group," said Bob D.

"I am connected to you, and you are connected to me," said

Opal M. "You are part of my sobriety. I can celebrate my sobriety each day with you."

How Others Came To Believe

A lot of us were not unbelievers. As children, we were brought up to believe in a Supreme Being, but that belief got rusty from lack of use, or we became disillusioned and dropped out along the way. The Supreme Being turned its back on us, we felt, or we walked away from it. With us, in order to grow spiritually, we had to find a way to learn to believe again.

Here is what others among us have to say about coming to believe:

"I am so glad I didn't have to believe anything when I first came in," said Dina T. "They let me find my own way. I thank God that he chose to remain anonymous in the beginning."

"I used to hear people say, 'Let God do it,' and I would say, 'Oh, throw up!'" said Tracy T. "But now it has happened to me—I say it myself."

"When I was a child, I had an imaginary friend I used to talk to all the time," said Marcia T. "Nobody could see her but me. I find now that I am beginning to do the same thing with my Higher Power—she is becoming my imaginary friend."

"I have this push-pull relationship with God," said Ted S. "I know I need help, but leave me alone—don't touch me. I know there is a God, but I don't want to talk to him right now. I can't trust my thinking; I just have to show up, stick with the group, and let it work. It doesn't work when I wall myself off from people."

"When I'm in trouble, I say, 'Maybe there's a power greater than myself who can handle this situation—and I think I'll let it,'" said Don S.

Six Stages of Coming To Believe

To point a direction, here are six things you can do to get started, six stages in the process which most of us went through, and what took place.

1. **Suspend judgment on spiritual matters.** When we could get past our rigid mind-set and look at this spiritual idea with an open mind, things started happening for us.

2. **Admit that such a Power might possibly exist.** As we conceded that there just might be some mysterious Guiding Presence behind everything, we started to feel the first indications of power coming into us.

3. **Accept that your own concept is all you need.** However hazy and ill-formed it might seem, our own personal concept of what this Guiding Presence might be is enough to begin to access it.

4. **Affirm that you want to make a connection.** As we kept returning to our concept, we started to experience the beginnings of spiritual feelings, and feel that we had made a real connection with our Higher Power.

5. **Trust the process.** We began to feel sure that there is some kind of dynamic power going on behind everything. We knew that there are no coincidences, that it all happens according to some kind of mysterious plan.

6. **Seek a close relationship with your Higher Power.** Our belief got stronger as we saw others working out their problems by depending on their Power Source. Then we accepted that we, too, had finally begun to find our power, and were forming a close relationship with our own Higher Power.

RESTORING US TO SANITY

"I had been diagnosed as manic-depressive, borderline schizoid and suicidal," said Sonja A. "Then when my psychiatrist told me I was an alcoholic, it was the best news I ever had."

While you are still dealing with the coming to believe process, the Second Step suggests that this power greater than yourself could restore you to sanity. "Whoa! Are they saying I am crazy?" you may think.

Quite a few of us have a lot of trouble with this phrase in Step Two. We immediately look at the other side of the coin, the term insanity, and we hang up there. It is easy to say to ourselves, "I wasn't really insane," and do a cop-out on this step.

"My sponsor told me, 'Put Step One away for a while and work on Step Two—you're so crazy, so stuck in your insanity, you can't comprehend Step One right now,'" said Ronnie P.

Defining Sanity

"The power of this program is that we are not all crazy at the same time," said Josh R.

Look up in your own dictionary the definition of the word *sanity* or the stem word *sane*. You will likely find that it means, among other things, *sound healthy thinking and behavior, the ability to manage one's own affairs.* Ask yourself: "When I was drinking and using, was my conduct characterized by sound, healthy thinking?"

If you have difficulty applying this part of the step to yourself, go back to Step One and review the writings you did on the subjects of powerlessness and unmanageability. Study your behavior then. Equate your behavior with sanity—or lack of it. You may find some clues there.

"You can argue about sanity," said Gregory G., "but when somebody or something kicks you in the crotch often enough, you ought to stay away from there if you have any sense. Go where the love is; stay where the love is." Yet, drinking and drugging, we kept coming back for more punishment. Our experiences in and out of sanity are sometimes sad, sometimes funny:

"What happened when I sobered up," said Steven F., "was that I became a lunatic. Sober, I couldn't even hold a job. It took six months before I could acquire the basic social skills, thanks to this program. What social skills I had before came from a bottle and a needle. That was my idea of sanity then."

"One day I decided to commit suicide," said Allie M. "I got

everything ready, then thought I would lie down a few moments to get calm before I killed myself. I woke up three hours later. I learned I didn't really want to commit suicide, I just needed a good nap."

Your Sanity Monitor: Your Sponsor

"My sponsor told me, 'Debbie, if you want to grow and develop in your life, then you must be willing to give up something you are really comfortable with, really familiar with,'" said Debbie G.

"'What's that?' I asked.

"'Insanity,' she said."

If you haven't already done so, you need to get a sponsor, because a good tight relationship with a sponsor can help you thrive in your program. A sponsor is an older, wiser teacher and friend who has traveled down the road before you. Good sponsors will keep you in their heart; they will be concerned with your sobriety, your welfare and your growth as a human being.

"Find people who, when they talk, you'll look up to and say, 'Wow!'" said Lynn C. "Those are the people who will help you on your way, and they will be put in front of you. Whoever is right will just appear.

"If you get one of these people who comes up to you and says, 'I'm going to be your sponsor,' then you might as well just live with that for just a little while. Because they are there for a reason. You're allowed to fire sponsors, you're allowed to outgrow sponsors, but you can't turn away any teachers, because you don't know enough."

Sponsors will be there for you, in person or by phone, to hear your problems, share their related experience with you, and steer you toward sane thinking and sane behavior. They will love you, but they won't coddle you. Part of their job is to tell you things you don't want to hear.

THE POWER IN STEP TWO

The power in Step Two is the transformation that takes place inside us, and the amazing things that start to happen in our lives, as a belief in a personal Higher Power kicks in. The restoration of sanity is the evidence of power channeling into us from our Higher Power.

"We tend to negate the power because it comes so gently," said Josh R.

We are becoming someone else, and the power is leading us there. From being a person who is often withdrawn, defiant and cynical, we are becoming a person who is more open to other people and other ideas. We are growing more loving and caring. We are developing a faith in our Higher Power and in ourselves. We are beginning to make changes in our lives.

"My power to change myself and to change my life is only limited by my belief," said Amy F.

Actually, we always had this power in us. We just didn't see it clearly. We didn't use it properly. It was like some gift, a toy handed us that we abandoned somewhere and forgot about.

"The power that I thought I had, I lost," said André T. "I had that power when I was a child. The power is very real for any young person who is seeking something. This could not have come into me had I not worked through each step, one at a time, with as much sincerity as I possibly could have had at the time.

"I have just opened myself up to the spiritual world and chosen to live and grow on spiritual lines like those the program talks about. I am still growing, too. So many changes have taken place in my life. And all the changes that have happened in recovery have come from within.

"It is the Power, the Source that is available to anyone who seeks it. I have found a power by which I could live. That is exactly what the steps are about. To me, it is a short-cut to God. Now, I let him show me how to live life, because I couldn't do it on my own. That's the bottom line for me. I couldn't do it, and he could."

Writing a Letter to Your Higher Power

Dennis P., as he marked thirty days of sobriety, shared with his group a letter he had written to his Higher Power:

"I am a troubled person, but I am worthy. My heart and soul are heavy. With your compassion and love, the sadness will be lifted. Only your power can remove the poison from my body. I don't know if I can give you all of me right now, but as I turn myself over to you one piece at a time, will you accept me? Do you think you could love me on that basis? I think you will, and somehow I feel better. Yours, Dennis."

This could be a good way for you to ease into working your Second Step without going beyond your comfort level. In a notebook, try writing a short letter from you to your own conception of a power greater than yourself. It may help you to crystallize what you believe and what you do not believe.

Chapter Three

CONNECTING WITH THE POWER

"My God as I understand God is not God as my mother understands Him. And that's okay."
—Victoria M.

Third Step: Made a decision to turn our will and our lives over to the care of God *as we understood Him.*

"I was taught by nuns," said Carmen C. "It always frightened me when Sister Alicia would punish me, then shake her finger at me and say, 'God is on my side!' It was a terrible thing to do to a child. I believed that for years—that God was not on my side. In the Third Step, I could not turn my will and my life over to that God. I had to develop a whole new concept of a loving God who was on my side."

The Third Step is really about breaking down the door that has been separating us from God—from him, from her or from it, whatever we may or may not understand God to be. Some of us have to take the door apart, piece by piece. Like Carmen, the last thing we do in working the Third Step is to turn our will and our lives over to the care of God. Why? Because we may need to do a lot of work before we can reach that point.

The Big Book states on page 68: "We never apologize for God," which is great if you have a strong faith. But we were afraid, most of us, afraid to turn anything over to the care of a Powerful Being whom we feared and didn't trust. It was hard to make a decision about something we didn't understand.

"I can't understand God—he's bigger than me," said Bruce O.

"A secret fear blocks my relationship with God," said Clark H. "I'm afraid that if I turn to God, he's going to make me become a priest and ship me off to do missionary work in China."

"I was afraid that God would make me become a Mother Teresa," said Susan L. "But he already had a Mother Teresa. What he doesn't have is a fully developed Susan, and I know that is what he wants."

Right - Gril

Spiritually Shy

As spiritually reserved alcoholics and addicts, we may need to revise our ideas of who or what God is. That is the first reason why making the decision about God in the Third Step is down the line a bit.

The second reason is that there is a dark aspect to this Third Step that is not revealed in the actual wording of the step. This somber side of the step is clearly described in the text on pages 60-63 in the Big Book. It gives us the clues to understand just why we need to turn our will and our lives over.

Some of us are just not ready for the rigorous self-appraisal called for in the first part of the Third Step. We slide past it into the God part, which may be scary enough, but not as scary as the self-evaluation. This is because the shadow side of the step requires us to look deep within ourselves and examine some of the mean and selfish character defects that have been hiding inside us. The aim of all this is to get us to really see how our pre-occupation with our own selves has caused many of our problems.

Taking the Step Apart

"Working the Third Step is like buying a new car," said Jeff R. "There is an awful lot to do before you can drive it away."

To help you to grasp the step, we break it down into component phrases, and we slightly modify the words. We deliberately take some phrases out of sequence. For example, it seems to make sense to discuss "God as we understand Him" before deciding to make a decision to turn our will and our lives over to the care of a God we may not understand at all.

TURNING IT OVER

"Early in my sobriety," said Dick E., "I told the man who later became my sponsor that I was afraid, and that no way was I going to turn my will and my life over to anybody or anything. He looked at me disgustedly and said, 'Knowing your history, Dick, if I were you, I'd turn my will and my life over to anybody who would take it.'"

Dick's reaction is typical. Fear is the dominant emotion that stops us in this step. Paradoxically, when we bridge the gap and place our lives in the care of this Higher Power, fear often takes a back seat in our lives.

"My fear was that I would turn it over and it wouldn't be received," said John A.

Cautiously we may ask, "What does it mean, 'turning it over'? Just how do you do that?"

What Turning It Over Means

"When I first came in, they kept saying to me, 'Turn it over! Turn it over!'" said Cliff C. "I didn't know what they were talking about. They might as well have been saying to me, 'Speak Italian! Speak Italian!'"

"People would tell me when I was new, 'Turn it over, George,'" said George C. "I thought they meant to flip something over, the way you turn over an egg in a frying pan."

Cliff and George learned that turning it over means to mentally release your hold on something, to give something over—like handing over your will, handing over your life, or your addiction, or any other big problem—to the care of your Spiritual Sponsor. It is an act of faith.

"When I think of turning it over and putting it into God's hands, I think of the Allstate Life Insurance TV commercials when I was growing up, where the cupped hands take it up and up, and it goes out of sight," said Sherry R.

What Letting Go Means

"Everything I let go of has claw marks on it," said Diane S.

The term "letting go" comes from the slogan, "Let go and let God." Letting go really means: "Turn it loose!" We stop trying to call the shots ourselves, we stop trying to manipulate the outcome of a situation. We let Higher Power take over. It's another way of saying, "Turn it over."

YOUR WILL AND YOUR LIFE

In working this step, the reason we don't leap right to the decision is because the Big Book and the TWELVE STEPS AND TWELVE TRADITIONS make it quite plain that the Third Step is very much about self-will—our excessive preoccupation with our own selves. Yet this aspect of the step is not made clear in the actual wording of the step. It sometimes tends to get lost in meetings when the discussion centers around turning our wills and our lives over. We don't always look at *why* we need to turn them over.

The Hidden Agenda

The why of it is this: We have another untreated addiction we haven't yet dealt with: our obsession with self, our own self. This self-will is the will we are supposed to turn over in this step. One dictionary defines *will* this way: *"The faculty by which the rational mind makes choices of its ends of action...."* Boil this down to: "rational mind ... makes choices ... action." That's what will does.

But when drinking and drugging, we turned our wills and our lives over to the care of chemical substances. It was our chemically juiced-up minds and our self-centered wills that kept making the wrong choices and triggering the wrong actions. What we are turning over in the Third Step is the kind of arrogant, self-centered thinking that nearly destroyed us—our will—and our blown-up sense of our own self-importance.

"I took my life far too personally," said Edward B. "My life is not as big a deal as I make it out to be."

Nevertheless, in the beginning, most of us hesitate about turning our lives over to the care of God. It may help us if we can understand one of the definitions of *life*: *"That which tends toward growth, development and progress; energy; animation; vigor."* That is not exactly how our lives felt when we were falling apart, right? Perhaps it is high time we thought about turning our lives over to the care of a wise, understanding Somebody who could do a better job than we did.

The Problems We Face

"In my self-centeredness, I wanted a God that could snap fingers and get things done in a hurry, the way I wanted them to go," said Charlie G.

This obsession with self is spelled out, flaw by flaw, in the Big Book's text on the Third Step on pages 60 through 62. It diagnoses the thinking and behavior patterns which caused us so much grief. As we study these word portraits of the addictive personality, as we turn inward and recognize ourselves in them, it is this confrontation with ourselves that may lead us to turn to a power greater than ourselves for help.

When we find ourselves identifying with these personality disasters, what it adds up to is that we have big problems. If you felt yourself relating to them, you probably need to examine the possibility that:

1. **You have a control problem.** We are always trying to tell people what to do, when to do it and how to do it—our way. Do you do this?

2. **You have a problem with selfishness.** We want more, want it all, and want it now. "Where's mine?" is our motto. Do you do this?

3. **You have a problem with self-centeredness.** We are interested only in ourselves, our achievements and our possessions. Are you like this?

4. **You have a problem with fear.** Fear cripples us, makes us shut down and isolate, and causes many of our problems. Does fear do this to you?

5. **You have a problem with self-delusion.** We con ourselves, see things the way we want to see them, not as they actually are. Do you do this?

6. **You have a problem with self-seeking.** We climb over anybody to get what we want. "What's in it for me?" is our yardstick. Is this you?

7. **You have a problem with self-pity.** The world is against us; everything goes wrong for us. Nobody values us. Do you feel this way?

8. **You have a problem with trying to play God.** We know absolutely what is best for people, and we tell them so. Are you like this?

9. **You have a human relations problem.** We have a tough time maintaining a close relationship with anybody. Is this true of you?

10. **You have a spiritual problem.** We are so arrogant and willful that we are unable to say, "Okay, God, let's try it your way." Is this you?

In the Third Step prayer on page 63 of the Big Book, we pray to be relieved of the "bondage of self" described in these ten problems. We must find a way to get rid of this selfishness, or it may eventually kill us. The Twelve Steps are designed to help us do this.

Self-Will Unzipped

The classic texts on Step Three call our attention to "self-will run riot." A dictionary defines the word *self-will* as a *willful or obstinate persistence in following our own desires or opinions.*

That means stubbornly insisting on having our own way. To *run riot* means *to resort to violence, disorder, disputes, quarrels, and debauchery or loose living.* Sound familiar? Most alcoholics and addicts are good at these things.

As we get into this Third Step work, we need to take a hard, honest look at the little monster living inside each one of us: ego freak, fear freak, control freak, selfish, self-centered, totally obsessed with Number One, very into self-delusion and self-pity—a self we would rather not recognize.

But recognize it we must, because zipping open this body bag and seeing what is inside is essential to knowing who we really are. However, doing this self-examination only in our heads is not enough. We must dig into it at gut level and see how it affects people we love and people we work with. Why are we asked to do all this? Because the final decision we make at the end of this step is a wrap-up—the conclusion of a process. After doing this unpleasant number on ourselves, we can then understand why we may be ready to lay the whole smelly package at God's doorstep and say, "You take it, H. P., I can't handle it."

The Solution to the Problem

"I will go to any length to do it my way," said Cliff C. "I think I always have to fix it myself. When it doesn't work, I finally remember, 'Oh, yeah!—turn it over.'"

The solution is simply to stop playing God. To begin to connect with the God that you might understand, you need to decide: 1) That you no longer want to live such a selfish, self-centered, self-willed, self-pitying, self-deluding life, and 2) that you need help and are about ready to consider turning your case over to the care of a Power who can put your life back in order.

"I often use a short prayer," said Susan L., "which goes like this: 'God, save me from myself.'"

GOD AS WE UNDERSTAND GOD

The ancient religious writers tell us that God made man in God's own image. Maybe, instead, man made God in man's own image, with all man's own emotions, including anger, jealousy and vengeance, along with frightening things such as threats, punishment and damnation. Perhaps that is why so many of us shied away and stayed scared of God. Now it may be time to do an overhaul of this idea and discover a new perception of a loving, caring Spiritual Parent that many of us longed for. Who knows?—the Great Spirit might appreciate a better image.

Invent Your Own God

"This is the only spiritual program in the world in which you can invent your own God—really invent Him! Man, you can make him any way you like!" said Tony C.

Yes, you can do what Tony said: Make God any way you want. In inventing a God you can live with, you are taking a long stride toward making your decision to turn your will and your life over to God's care. You are making the first move in actively inviting God to become a part of your life.

In her story which opens this chapter, Carmen C. had difficulty with the God of her childhood. Your God, too, may have been a God who, you felt, was out to get you. Now, you can consign that God to the past. When you do, then you begin to find another God in your own head and own heart.

A God Who Dances

"I could only believe in a God who dances," wrote the German philosopher, Friedrich Nietzsche.

Maybe you'd like a God who goes dancing with you. Why not? You have the imagination and the creative ability to make up for yourself a God who will love you, dance with you, eat with you, sleep with you, and look out for your needs.

"My God is playful and frisky, and even a little naughty, like some kind of elf," said Barbara A. "I have a lot of fun with my God. We laugh a lot together."

You can sing with your God buddy. You can make God male or female, or both. If you liked sports in school, you can make God a sort of supernatural athletic coach who tells you what to do and when to do it, who coaches you in the game and cheers for you to win. You might imagine God in another role as the most powerful agent-manager in the universe, one who is going to handle your talent, show you how to get your act together, and manage your career.

"Now I talk very personally with my God," said Karen T. "When I go outside and see a lovely summer day with sunlight sparkling on everything, I say, 'Oh, you are so beautiful!' And my God has a great sense of humor. I may see something comical or think of something bizarre, and I will laugh out loud and say, 'Oh, you are so *funny!*'"

Hooking into the Power Source

"My sponsor nailed me on Step Three," said Matthew T. "He said to me, 'Every time you fly on an airplane, you turn your will and your life over to the care of an unknown airline pilot. So what is your particular problem about doing this with God?' I couldn't answer him. That's what got me started on the Third Step."

In the Big Book, we read about God as being all-powerful. We comprehend that God is the Source of Power. This is where the power is. But we never experience the power until we connect with it. The point is, we don't really have to understand all about God—that is too big an order. Just a little understanding is enough to get us hooked in and powered up. For instance, we don't have to understand electricity to enjoy what it does for us. We just plug into it and let the power flow. It illuminates all the dark corners and makes everything work. By the same token, we don't have to understand TV. We just switch it on and enjoy the picture. The power is there, waiting. Essentially, this is what we do in Step Three. We connect. We attach, combine, couple, join, unite, bridge, link-up, span the space between us and God. And as the juice flows into us, it begins to light up our lives. We are up, on line and running. That is when we begin to get our deeper understanding and appreciation of God.

TO THE CARE OF GOD

"When I think how many times I turned my will and my life over to the care of other people," said Betty C., "I think, 'So what is the big deal? Why not give God a chance at it?'"

It is in this third phrase, *to the care of God*, that people often miss the point of the Third Step. They read this part of the step the wrong way. They incorrectly see it, and say it, as "turn our will and our lives over to God." It does not say that. They omit the meaningful phrase "the care of."

The Great Caregiver

Those three words are important to the sense of the step. We turn our will and our lives over to *the care of* God. The difference is this: You do not give up your will and your life. You simply place them in God's care, and under God's protection and guidance. You can take them back any time.

"God never over-rules my own free will," said Frank Y. "If I take a step of commitment to him, I can always back off. He never enslaves you. He never rapes you."

Consider this comparison: Some of the richest men in the world got that way by turning their fortunes over to the care of wise investment counselors. They never gave away their money. It was invested for them. It remained theirs. They got it back, with interest, when they wanted it.

We turn our Camaro over to the care of valet parking. We get it back. We turn our Rolex over to the care of watch repair. It's still ours. We turn our child over to the care of a good day care center. It's still our baby. We turn our will and our lives over to the care of a surgeon when we have an operation. When we come out of the anesthetic, we get them back.

Could it be so different when we turn our will and our lives over to the care of God? When we do this, we are counting on God to be our caregiver, and we are trusting God to keep us on target in all our affairs.

"I have to trust my God, then I have to trust the God that is in me—which is the same thing," said Marvin L.

THE POWER IN STEP THREE

We know that risk-taking often has great rewards. Think of it this way: In a business deal or a life crisis, suppose there was a powerful ally whom you didn't know too well, but who had a fine reputation. This individual had watched you and your performance, and was willing to go all out for you. Wouldn't it be worth taking a chance to get this ally in your corner?

Your Power Partner

The bottom line is really about deciding to go into partnership—joining forces with a partner who has a lot more power than you have. It is a partner who has infinite resources. It is a partner who is far more knowledgeable and experienced in life than you are. It is a partner who will steer you through tough times and help you make the right decisions. It is a partner who will reward you well and, despite that awesome power, will always treat you with tenderness and affection. Would you go for such a deal?

The Power in One-Ness

In the First Step, we studied a section subtitled, "The Power in 'We.'" That was about the power and strength we draw from feeling part of the group. Now, in the Third Step, comes a much deeper meaning of the power in We. If you make the transition to becoming a partner with God, with you and God it now becomes

We—God and you. Two become united: We are One. When it happens, we discover the power and joy in our One-ness with God.

MAKING THE DECISION

In making your decision, you are making a power move. With your eyes wide open, you are choosing to go into a committed relationship. It may feel like taking a big risk. But in order to connect, we risk it and say, "Yes! I will make the commitment. I am going to go with this thing and decide now to turn my will and my life over to the care of God *as I understand God*! God help me!"

Actually, making a decision usually simplifies our lives. Because once we have made a decision about one big issue, then a lot of little decisions make themselves almost automatically. They simply follow the path laid out by the big decision. This is true in any area of our lives: deciding on a lifestyle or a career, deciding to get married—or deciding on a God. Make the main decision and everything else falls into place.

A Leap of Faith

"I heard a noise in the kitchen, and turned to see my two-year-old son on top of the kitchen counter, teetering at the edge," said Mike G. "My heart almost stopped. 'Daddy!' he called, and stretched out his arms and leaped into space. I lunged forward and caught him in my arms. Later I thought: 'He had no fear of falling. He never doubted for an instant that I would catch him. How wonderful!' I thought, 'A true leap of faith. If only I could make such a leap of faith to my God.'"

You, like Mike's little boy, may have the courage to go ahead and make that leap of faith. But even if you still have doubts, go ahead and risk it. "If you don't believe it, do it anyway," said Bill T.

Feeling follows action, according to William James, the

American philosopher. What James meant was: As you make the decision, as you take the action, the feeling generally follows on the heels of the action. Once you take action on your decision, something seems to quietly click. Like loading a software program into a computer, God becomes loaded into your consciousness, and the power is always there for you to access.

Align Your Will with God's

Have a go at this simple gesture—it may serve as an affirmation of your decision to turn your will and your life over to the care of God. Hold your hands straight out, index fingers pointed forward, other fingers and thumbs curled into your palm. Slowly bring the index fingers closer together until they are side by side, touching. Think of them as God's will and your will, in perfect alignment with each other. Whenever it comes to mind, make this quick demonstration to affirm your oneness with God.

Look to Part Two of this book, in the Work Plan for Step Three, for other exercises that will lead you through Step Three.

"When you make the decision to let everything go and turn it all over to God's care, that generates tremendous power," said Jack G. "That's when things started happening for me."

Chapter Four

WHO YOU REALLY ARE

*"Get out of your head and get into your gut.
Then you'll begin to get the answers you need
in the Fourth Step."*–Jan C.

**Fourth Step: Made a searching and fearless moral inventory
of ourselves.**

"My sponsor told me, 'Drugs and alcohol did not get you into
trouble, Paul; you got yourself into trouble,'" said Paul G. "Then
he told me, 'You don't have an alcohol and drug problem. What
you have is a big Paul problem.' That got my attention and got
me into my Fourth Step inventory."

The Fourth Step requires us to face up to the troublesome side
of our natures and get ready to do something about it. People
tend to dread doing Step Four because they think it's hard. It is.
The good news is that if you have done a good self-appraisal in
your work on the First Step and the first part of the Third Step,
you're partway there.

For more than half a century, the experience of A. A. indicates
strongly that if we don't do a thorough Fourth Step we are likely
to pick up a drink and be back into our addictions again.
Basically, what the Fourth Step asks us to do is to review our
lives and make out six lists based on our feelings and actions.
The reason we work this step is to clean house, mentally and
emotionally, so we can begin to get rid of the mistakes of our
past. We clean house room by room. We clean house issue by
issue.

"I loved doing my Fourth Step," said Ramona C. "I was so self-centered it was wonderful to be able to concentrate entirely on myself and have everybody approve my doing it."

The Power in the Fourth Step

"Until you have done an honest and thorough Fourth Step," said Jack G., "you don't even know who the hell you really are."

The power in the Fourth Step comes from recognizing at last the mistakes and personality defects that have caused us a lot of pain. The power is in the depth of self-knowledge that we acquire. This power is linked to the corrective actions which this step and the Fifth Step suggest we take, actions which are mostly contrary to our compulsive-addictive instincts and beliefs. We procrastinate, we resist taking the actions because it means work and changing. Many times we have to be so stressed out by feelings or events that we are forced into action to get relief. Then we are amazed when it actually works, when the pain eases, and when the feeling of euphoria takes over.

Marie E.'s Experience

"When I came to the Fourth and Fifth Steps," said Marie E., "I looked at them and I said, 'Unh-unh. There are some things that I will never tell anyone.'

"So I had been sober about a year when I hit an emotional bottom. It got so painful that I was either going to drink again or I had to move forward in the recovery program. Luckily, a woman who became my second sponsor took me aside and said, 'You have to make a decision. Either you drink again or you get started on your Fourth Step.'

"It was really that simple. I was petrified to drink again; I didn't know if I would have a second chance to come back to Alcoholics Anonymous. And she said, 'Besides, what have you got to lose?'

"That statement really hit me. I said, 'If it doesn't work, then I just go drink. But if it works—and it just might—then I have a chance.' So I did my Fourth Step and a Fifth Step. And that was really a turning point for me."

An Overview

To give you an idea of what the Fourth Step entails, here is an outline of the work you will be doing if you choose to go ahead and work the step.

1. **Resentments.** You search out and examine your resentments, describe them, list them, and tell how they impacted your life.

2. **Your fears.** You recall and then list all the fears and phobias you may have, and try to analyze each of these fears.

3. **Your sex behavior.** You review your sex conduct. You write about each episode to determine people you harmed in your sexual activities.

4. **Emotional and economic security/insecurity.** You analyze your personal relationships. You survey the extent to which domination and control issues, and concern for financial stability, may have been harmful to you and others.

5. **Your mistakes, faults, character defects.** You go back to the resentments list, identify where you were wrong and why you were wrong.

6. **Your assets.** You look at the good qualities that are part of your makeup, and you make a list of these assets.

A Searching and Fearless Inventory

"If you haven't worked a thorough Third Step, you are not ready to take a Fourth Step," said Tomas C. "Unless you have really turned it over, you cannot be fearless in your inventory."

Every instinct in us rebels at doing this disagreeable work. We are afraid of what we might find. This inventory is taking stock of yourself, just like taking stock of merchandise in a store. You examine everything in stock and list it. The good stuff you keep. The bad stuff, you decide to clear out. "I'm very familiar with inventories," said Cliff C. "When I was a child they took my inventory every day."

What Is a Moral Inventory?

It is called a *moral* inventory, not an *immoral* inventory. *Moral* means simply the principles of right and wrong, a standard of right behavior. We have to see what we did right and what we did wrong, and figure out why we did it. But first, we have to get totally honest with ourselves.

We want to be honest—but, still, aren't there some secrets that are better left alone? No. If you do not acknowledge your secrets in your Fourth Step and share them in your Fifth Step, you will almost certainly have to do it over—do another Fourth Step at a later date to clean up unfinished business.

Instincts Running Wild

"Unless you have some sense of guilt and shame," said Jim D., "it is almost impossible to work a Fourth Step."

In the Third Step we learned about self-will run riot. In the Fourth Step we learn about our basic human instincts going ape—it's the same disease, just a different flare-up. Often, when we examine an episode on one of our inventory lists, behind the incident we find one of our fundamental life desires or hungers: the need for sex, the need for love and intimate companionship, the ambition to acquire material things, or the drive to be financially successful and emotionally safe—all socially acceptable urges.

But the problem with the alcoholic and addict is one of excess. We went overboard. Our instincts ran away with us. At times we became slaves to our instincts. When we kept grabbing more of a good thing, we lost our sense of balance and got into trouble. In our inventories, we need to get specific about patterns of behavior like this.

"Too much was never enough," said Leslie D.

FIVE WAYS TO APPROACH THE STEP

"You don't take a Fourth Step in your head," said Bill P. "That doesn't cut it. You take a Fourth Step in writing, on paper."

Here are five approaches to doing a Fourth Step. All of them work.

It doesn't matter what method you choose to follow as long as you get it all written out. Then, from what you have written, you can make up your inventory lists. A word of caution: Don't leave your Fourth Step lying around on a desk or in a drawer. Even the best of people are curious.

The Classic Way

Hundreds of thousands of people have done their Fourth Steps following the Big Book suggestion beginning at the bottom of page 63. On page 65, it recommends making up a chart with three columns for listing resentments, causes, and effects on you. The text then leads into other areas to be inventoried. This method is straightforward and time-tested.

The Crash Deadline Way

"One Sunday night at a meeting I asked a guy to be my sponsor," said Hans W. "He told me, 'I've listened to you in meetings and I know where you're at. You're stuck in your Fourth Step, right?' I admitted I was.

"'If I sponsor you,' he said, 'we will take the Fifth Step together this coming Thursday. That gives you three days to do your Fourth Step. I don't care how much you write, but bring me only one sheet of paper with your inventory outlined on two sides of the paper. That's it. You will talk it, not read it. Okay?'

"That's how I did my first Fourth. I didn't get much sleep that week, but it's a great way to do it. It sets a deadline, makes it a top priority, and you get it done. I needed a tough sponsor like that to get me off my butt."

The Journaling Method

Buy an $8^1/_2$-inch by 11-inch wire-bound notebook. Each day, as you remember important incidents about people, places and things in your life, write for a while in your Fourth Step journal. Toward the back of the book, enter the title of each one of your lists on separate pages. As you reread and process what you have written, transfer incidents to the appropriate list. This is a steady, unhurried method that gives you time for reflection and insights.

The Tape Recorder Way

"I have a problem with reading and writing," said Dusty G. "My second sponsor told me to list the names of the significant people in my life, and then just talk into my hand-held tape recorder about how I felt about them then, and how I feel about them now.

"I did that, and taped it on two cassettes. Taking my Fifth Step with my sponsor, we would listen to the tape, stop the recorder, talk it through and relate it to one of the inventory lists. He spotted the character defects behind most of these actions and made me understand them. He helped me write out the lists of defects and assets."

The Work Plan

In Part Two of this book, a Work Plan suggests study assignments, instructions, exercises and examples of inventory situations. It will lead you directly into your inventory lists. If you like a structured method, go with it.

MAKING THE LISTS

Whatever method you may choose, it will help you to understand what is going on if you can break down the stuff you have written into different categories of inventories. In addition to this, the raw data, the incidents from your life which you list, goes nowhere unless you analyze it. This is the real meat in the Fourth

Step. It leads us to the reasons why we did some of these harmful things, and opens the way for getting them out of our lives.

Start with the Resentments List

"Holding a resentment against somebody is like drinking a cup of poison and sitting there waiting for the other person to die," said Billy H.

What, precisely, is a resentment? A resentment is an *indignant sense of injury or insult,* according to the dictionary. The word stems from the French verb, *sentir,* which means *to feel or experience*. Putting a *re* at the beginning of the word, as in *resentir,* suggests that we refeel the injury again and again.

While the Fourth Step is about the damage we caused others, it is also very much about the reality of the many people who dominated us, hurt us and caused resentments in us. As a result, we became bitter and stayed angry.

"When I let myself get into resentments, I get the same feeling I got when I was drunk," said Ted S. "I say, 'See, life is not fair.' If I stay that way long enough, then I start to get insane and paranoid, and I get closer and closer to a drunk. I get emotionally drunk."

When we harbor resentment, we keep the injury alive. Some of us never let go. We clutch resentments to us, keep rehashing them all our lives.

"When I am in resentment, I am chained in the past," said Rita Y. "In fear, I am locked into the future. No way am I living in the present."

People who nurse resentments often get sick. These old hurts take a toll on our minds, our physical systems and wreck our spiritual well-being.

"Resentment," claims the Big Book on page 64, "is the 'number one' offender. It destroys more alcoholics than anything else."

What to do: Look backward through your life and identify the people, the rules and the institutions that hurt you or made you mad. Write down the name of the offender and write down why you feel the resentment. Then pinpoint the emotion it arouses in you—fear, anger, guilt, jealousy, and the like—and write that down. Finally, put down where it affects your life—your self-image, your sex life, your finances.

The Big One: Fear

"I found out through taking a Fourth and Fifth Step that what motivated my life was fear," said Nancy L. "And I didn't know this. But if I continue to make decisions based on my fears, all of those fears will come true."

Like alcohol and drugs, fear is a common denominator among all alcoholics and addicts. Fears eat away at our souls as well as at our ability to get things done. The Big Book nailed it on page 62, when it said that alcoholics are "Driven by a hundred forms of fear ..."

"I was afraid of fear—I generate my own fear," said Ross N. "I had to learn to feel the fear, to experience it. But when I write about the fears, when I talk to somebody about them, they lose their power."

"I was finally able to deal with my fear of authority figures by not putting my father's face on my boss, not putting my father's face on my sponsor, on the postman, or anyone else," said Ted B.

What to do: In your inventory of fears, root out each fear in yourself, write it down and put a name tag on it. Then ask yourself: "Why did I feel threatened? Why do I have this fear?" Figure out how it impacts your life.

Your Sex List

"When you're in a heavy sexual relationship, you tend to lose your brains," said Elizabeth I. "And when alcohol and drugs are part of the scene, you are really crazy."

Your sex list is not about what you did, how you did it, and how many times you did it. It is about whom you hurt in doing it, and how you hurt yourself. When we put our sex drives out front, nothing could stand in the way of getting them satisfied. And our choices weren't always smart.

"I was attracted to toxic relationships the same way I was attracted to toxic chemicals," said Leroy C.

Today, people have multiple relationships, going from one partner to another. And people marry and divorce a lot today.

"I was married eight times to five different women," said Dave N. "In the six years I've been sober, I haven't found it necessary to take a drink of alcohol, take a drug, or get married."

Concerning sex, the Big Book says on page 69, "We all have sex problems." And the TWELVE STEPS AND TWELVE TRADITIONS lays it on the line on page 54: "The primary fact that we fail to recognize is our total inability to form a true partnership with another human being."

Perhaps one reason for this fact is that losing ourselves in sex can be simply one more form of escape for the alcoholic and the addict. With us, sex may be just another exciting way to anesthetize other feelings, a way to push them into the background for a while and get a feelings fix. Sex can become as addictive as any other form of escape.

Part of the problem for alcoholics and addicts may be that it is our nature to be selfish. So with us, sex can be a totally self-centered activity, and we don't always give much consideration to our partners' emotional needs.

"Nobody stayed long in any of my relationships," said Martha Y. "My attitude was, 'Get it right the first time, or get out.' Mostly they got out."

"I don't take lovers, I take hostages," said Stanley J.

What to do: You list the partners. You spell out what happened, who got hurt, how they got hurt and why, where you were wrong, and the trouble that resulted. Some questions in the Work Plan for Step Four may help you. If your sexual orientation is gay male or lesbian, it is part of who you are, and it belongs here. If you are bisexual, write about it. If you are homophobic—admit it here. If you were the victim or the perpetrator of sexual abuse, put it down—it goes in your inventory.

Emotional Security/Insecurity

"I liked anger. I could control people with my anger," said Sally B.

Rarely is the alcoholic or addict emotionally secure. How can we be when we are so often filled with resentment, anger and fear?

Adding to the situation, we are frequently at odds with our families. So there is little feeling of security on that score. Many times our only gauge of personal security is our identity in a relationship or marriage.

We seem to be always seeking to find ourselves in someone else. Yet, moving into a relationship or marriage, sometimes we tend to dominate the partner and cut him or her off from the world with our jealousy. Unless we are in control of the situation, we feel threatened.

On the other hand, some of us are so dependent that we fool ourselves into thinking that as long as we are hooked up with another person, and the sex is great, we are safe and things are okay. But it is not okay when we allow ourselves to be dominated by the other person. We clamp down on our emotions, become people pleasers, and settle for peace at any price.

"I was a people pleaser," said Colette T. "The trouble was, not many people were pleased."

When the partner grows tired of our clinging dependency, the relationship frequently comes unglued; we fall apart and start desperately hunting for someone with whom we can set up the same situation again.

"I have always been half a person," said Gregory G. "I had to find another half-person to connect with. I had to have a grasp on one half-person and a grasp on a second half-person before I could let go of either one."

This inventory will take some deep searching to uncover the

intricacies of our interpersonal relations with others. We must see clearly how we use people, and how others use us, in an effort to prop up our fragile sense of security. Sometimes we may need to explore this portion of our inventory with a sponsor or a counselor before we can understand it and write about it.

What to do: You need to look at each interpersonal relationship that consistently caused, or causes, friction and turmoil in your life, and write about it. Here's a test to see if a situation is upsetting your emotional serenity:

1. Does it make you mad?
2. Do you brood a lot about it?
3. Does it make you feel gloomy and dejected?
4. Does it make you feel sorry for yourself?

Four yes answers indicate you may have a problem.

Business, Financial, Employment Security

"I was one of those who thought that if I still had checks left in my checkbook there must be money in the bank," said Marie E. "I almost ended up in jail for that one."

The real measure of your economic security is based on to what degree fear and worry about money have landed you in trouble in your financial affairs. The drive to be successful, look successful and acquire your share of worldly goods is a normal, admirable instinct. Yet some alcoholics and addicts push it too far. We defy all the laws.

Either we may be so careless about money that we are one step ahead of disaster, or we may be obsessively power-mad, driven to accumulate money and material things the way pill-heads stockpile their pills. Sometimes we can be compulsive shoppers, or credit card junkies, juggling balances between a dozen credit cards.

In doing your research on this inventory, accept the premise that practicing alcoholics and drug addicts become skilled liars and cheats. Dishonesty comes as naturally to us as breathing. We steal from parents, relatives, friends, clients or employers. We lie about money. We shoplift. We default on loans. We inflate expense accounts. When we have the opportunity, we manipulate money in dozens of ways to our own benefit.

What to do: This is the down-and-dirty part of our personal inventory. If you get real about the meaning of the word honesty, you will know exactly where to look for these mistakes and blemishes on your record. List the people and firms from whom you stole, or from whom you borrowed money and never paid it back. Put down the names of those you conned, swindled or double-crossed. Question all your motives.

Listing Character Defects

"All my character defects can be lumped under either self-centeredness or self-destruction," said Barry H.

What exactly are character defects? They are the negative aspects of our natures, the personality flaws and attitudes that cause us to act in ways which are hurtful to others and to ourselves.

Traditionally, the inventory of character defects is positioned right after the inventory list of resentments, but how can you really get a handle on the whole line of character defects until after you have examined your sexual behavior, your fears, your dishonesty about money, and the people you hurt?

Vengefulness, self-pity, pride, selfishness, fear, anger, arrogance, jealousy—these turn up on many lists of character defects. Greediness in all areas is a character defect with lots of us. It leads to going out of control, which leads to unmanageable lives—and we are right back where we started.

What to do: Closely analyze your various inventory lists to draw a bead on your character defects. Two questions to ask yourself are, "Exactly how did I contribute to the bad situation?" and "What flaw in my character was the real villain behind this?" Ask your sponsor to help you locate and identify your major faults.

Listing Your Assets

"I had to remember that a true balance sheet lists both assets and liabilities," said Burton V.

Now for the good part, figuring out your assets. You may already know some of them. If they feel sincere, don't question, just put them down. Study your other lists and see if you spot a situation where you were kind, compassionate and caring. Try to remember incidents where you went out of your way to help someone. Was there a time when you were generous—gave of yourself and gave of your money? You don't need to fill up a page or two. Six or eight honest ones are enough to make you feel good about yourself.

What to do: Seek outside help from people you trust, people who know you and like you. A sponsor is a good place to start.

The Bite-Size-Pieces Approach

Here's an alternate procedure, an exercise that will help you get a leg up on your Fourth Step inventorying. It is total simplicity and not scary at all. You feel you can handle it.

"The relaxed way to do your first Fourth Step," said sponsor Josh R., "is to take one sheet of paper and write out on it four things about yourself that bug you. Then talk them over with another person. That is a simple and adequate first Fourth Step. Save the paper. Do another paper when you feel like it. Save that paper, too. Later on, do another one. First thing you know, you have done a comprehensive Fourth Step."

"The Fourth Step is not about doing a hatchet job on yourself," said Cliff C. "It is about finding patterns of behavior. Do it with your sponsor first. Talk it through. Rehearse it. There is nothing negative about doing a Fourth Step."

Chapter Five

DUMPING YOUR GARBAGE

"I learned real humility taking my Fifth Step with my sponsor. I am just getting down to the really nasty stuff, and my sponsor yawns."—Ed L.

Fifth Step: Admitted to God, to ourselves, and to another human being the exact nature of our wrongs.

"When you get sick of being sick, you take the Fifth Step," said Sandra Z. "You claim your garbage. You own it. It stinks so bad you have to dump it. You unload it and give it to God and to another human being."

The Fifth Step is about blowing your cover, about telling somebody else who you really are. Trying to hide our secrets, we did a great cover-up job because our secrets made us feel ugly inside. In Step Four we worked to discover the obstacles that have been holding us back in our lives. We found our weak spots, identified what the trouble was, and pinpointed our character defects. Now, in Step Five, we admit the exact nature of our wrongs and prepare to get rid of them.

While it is the simplest of all the steps, it is probably the most feared. Its simplicity lies in the fact that little is required but to talk. The real work has already been done in Step Four. But unless we verbalize our Fourth Step inventory, it remains bottled up inside us and little good is accomplished.

The Purpose of the Fifth Step

The main reason for doing Step Five is to get rid of the messy remains of the past. Five is the action follow-up to Step Four: to get moving on the house-cleaning, we began to haul out the garbage and dump it at last. We do this when we declare our dirty work and confess it to ourselves, to a Higher Power, and to another person.

A Cop-Out

Acting from fear, it is easy to talk yourself into a cop-out by deciding to admit your wrongs just to yourself and to your Higher Power—just the two of you. It would be far less embarrassing to do it this way without having to confess it all to some other person. We think: "I know all about it, and God certainly knows all about it, so why involve a third party, right?"

Wrong, because your thinking may be scrambled by self-justification and unrealistic reasoning. You wouldn't tell it the way it really was. You wouldn't get the detached feedback you need from an experienced listener. Doing it that way, you are keeping it all in the closet. It has been there a long time, and it needs to come out. What's more, you will not have properly taken the step. You'll only have to face up and do it another time, and you will run a high risk of drinking and doping between times.

Feelings

"The gift of Step Five is the gift of being able to share, to spill it all out, to tell what you are feeling, what you are going through," said Sally B. Emotions may run high when doing this step. Getting started, fear is the overriding feeling—we fear disclosing our innermost secrets to someone.

"When I took my Fifth Step, I was so scared and ashamed, I had some stuff written in code up at the top of the page so nobody but me would know what it was," said Ginny J.

Guilt and pain creep over us when we admit the nasty things

we have done to others. When we lied to people we loved, or stole money or hurt them, we became ashamed to be around them. As we avoided them, feelings of separation and loneliness resulted. Now, a sense of humiliation hits us as we face the prospect of spelling out our wrongs to another human being. On top of these emotions, we often feel unworthy—we believe that people would hate us if they knew what goes on inside us.

"I asked my sponsor, 'Why do I feel so guilty?'" said Leslie D. "'Because you are guilty,' she said. 'How can I stop feeling so guilty?' I asked her. 'Stop doing the things that make you feel guilty,' she told me."

THE EXACT NATURE OF OUR WRONGS

"Hearing my Fifth Step, my sponsor pointed out a character defect I hadn't even put on my list: my guilt," said Clint O. "It was actually my main instrument of self-torture."

The step says *"wrongs,"* but in the first two paragraphs on page 72 in the Big Book dealing with the Fifth Step, it says "the exact nature of our *defects*" and "discussing our *defects* with another person." Wrongs, character defects, shortcomings—the terms seem to be used interchangeably in the Big Book, and this can at times be a little confusing.

However, the *exact nature* of something is its *precise and essential characteristic*. That means: What is the real essence of it? In this case, we have to look behind the actual wrong deed to accurately identify it. If you slapped somebody hard, the exact nature of it was physical violence or abuse. If you forced sex on an unwilling partner, the exact nature of it was rape. That is how we identify the exact nature of our wrong deeds.

"There is not a secret in my life that my sponsor doesn't know," said Eric L. "And he accepts me and loves me just the same. That is one great feeling."

Confession as Healing Therapy

"I stayed out of trouble by never telling anybody very much about myself," said Kevin R. "I had a tough time opening up in the Fifth Step."

The act of confession is as old as time. In ancient Greece, the citizens who had wronged men and offended the gods made the journey to consult the oracle at the temple of Apollo at Delphi. There, the deity could be accessed. They told their misdeeds to the priestess of the temple, were counseled about their futures, and were cleansed of their wrongdoing and were purified.

As a healing therapy, the custom of confession has continued down through the centuries to present-day sessions with clergy and psychiatrists. But most alcoholics and addicts lead a double life and are adept at non-disclosure and at lying to their therapists. The buck stops here in the Fifth Step: the step demands total honesty as we level with another human being.

"When I took my Fifth Step," said Ramona C., "I started going through my life as it was—not the way I pretended it was."

How Confession Helps You in Your Program

"I don't have a problem being alone," said Sally B., "I have a problem being with other people. Until I let you know who I am, I'm never going to heal."

In sharing our life story, heart-to-heart, no holds barred, with another human being, several benefits come to us that help us in our program of sobriety. Many people have reported these feelings after letting it all come out in their Fifth Step:

We get free of the sense of separateness, the feeling of being rejected and friendless. We develop the awareness that we really do belong. We feel closer to other men and women, and closer to our Supreme Being. We get the sensation that we are forgiven and that our forgiveness of others is possible. We become more humble, and we come to understand our inner selves much better.

We grow more aware of the value of counsel and guidance, and we are more open to accepting it.

ADMITTING TO YOURSELF

In the Fifth Step, you need to tell your story out loud to yourself. "What? Talking to myself?" That's exactly what it is. You need to hear yourself verbalizing it aloud, rather than just writing it and reading it in silence. You need to level with your Inner Guide. Your Inner Guide has known all along what was going on, of course. Now, your Spiritual Twin needs to hear it from you to know that you are no longer doing a head job on yourself. An agenda for taking this portion of the step with yourself appears in the Work Plan in Part Two.

ADMITTING TO GOD

"I didn't have to be good enough to earn God's love," said Tony C. "It was already there."

Admitting our wrongs to our God is a part of the step which some of us are inclined to skim over. We assume that our Spiritual Parent is already quite aware of what we have done. But we are trying to build a closer, bonding relationship with the God of our own understanding. So we cover all bases. We come clean to our Higher Power so that there are no secrets between us.

A visualization approach, suggested in the Work Plan for Step Five, may help you get into this intimate sharing with your Higher Power.

ADMITTING TO ANOTHER HUMAN BEING

"I have to get this stuff out," said Leslie D. "I have to talk, even though I am scared to talk to you. Other people don't understand. You do."

The one-on-one sharing with another person in Step Five is the beginning of trust for many of us. It is the start of reconnecting with the human race. When you share your secrets with someone else, who then reveals to you some secrets from his or her own past, you see yourself as not so terrible after all. The process of forgiving yourself begins.

Finding a Safe Listener

"My problem with the Fifth Step," said Susie N., "was not so much my lack of faith in God, but my lack of faith in another human being."

Finding a listener whom you can trust may be the toughest part of the step. It is recommended that you select someone who is familiar with Twelve Step programs and who has heard Fifth Steps before. A husband or wife is seldom a wise selection. If it feels right for you, a good choice might be a priest, minister or rabbi. Other possibilities: a doctor, psychiatrist, therapist or counselor. If he or she seems warm, compassionate and trustworthy, perhaps yes; if the individual seems cool and reserved, think twice.

"My Fifth Step bombed out," said Ted S. "It was an anti-climax. I took my Fifth with a rabbi in his office. I poured my heart out for an hour, told him every secret, my whole story. When it was over, he shook his head, stood up, and said, 'Well, that's too bad,' and showed me to the door."

Many of us take the step with our sponsors. If you have a well-developed, trusting relationship with a sponsor, consider that person.

Sharing Your Secrets

"Tell a Fifth Step," said sponsor Katherine R. "Do not read it. In telling it, the right thoughts come to you."

Let the setting be a place of the listening partner's choice. For example, one west coast sponsor always hears Fifth Steps in his car. In total privacy, they drive up the coastal highway for as long as it takes the sponsee to tell his story. Then they discuss it on the way home.

Set the day, the time and the place at the listener's convenience. Take with you to this session an outline of your Fourth Step inventory. Allow plenty of time, an hour, two hours or more. Then show up. Say a small prayer for guidance, glance at your notes, and start talking.

"In my Fifth Step," said Lisa M., "my sponsor told me, 'It's really very simple—you make it complicated in the telling because you don't want to take responsibility for it.'"

THE POWER IN THE FIFTH STEP

The power in Step Five is in the tremendous feeling of relief that comes over us when the secrets are finally shared, out in the open and defused. We experience a sense of release, a new freedom as we dump the guilt and shame of the past and let it all go.

The Power of Self-Acceptance

One of the powerful effects of a Fifth Step well done is the change that takes place in us from low self-esteem and self-hatred to a healthy self-acceptance. Negative self-images are replaced by strong feelings of self-worth. We begin to actually like ourselves.

Thirteen Power Benefits

After the exhilaration that follows the taking of a Fifth Step, it takes a little time to absorb some of the other benefits that come to us as a result. Some other things we may begin to experience:

- We are not afraid any longer.
- We are not ashamed of anything any longer.
- We feel more trusting of other people.
- We are completely comfortable being alone with ourselves.
- We frequently find that the urge to drink and drug is gone.
- We sense a new security in our sobriety.
- We personally experience what humility means.
- Our self-respect and serenity are restored.

• Old tapes are being replaced by the power of new thinking.
• We have a feeling of greater spiritual awareness.
• We feel a closer relationship with our Higher Power.
• We feel we may have something to give to others.
• We feel our Higher Power is guiding us in the right direction.

"I've learned that God not only loves me, God actually likes me," said Garner P. "I've learned I can lean on God."

Share One Deep Secret

If the thought of revealing everything about yourself to another person still terrifies you, then you can risk just a little bit to get the feel of a Fifth Step. Go to a dear friend whom you know, like and trust, or to your sponsor. Say, "I need to tell you something I've never told to another living soul," and then tell him or her about one dark secret—just one. Then discuss it.

See how you feel about it afterward. Chances are it won't seem so awful, once it's out. It may give you courage to do your Fifth Step.

"It's only in the emotional sharing of your deepest secrets," said Ila J., "that you destroy their destructive negative power over you You are free."

Chapter Six

BEATING A DEAD HORSE

*"My temper got me into trouble,
and my pride kept me there."*—Grita W.

Sixth Step: Were entirely ready to have God remove all these defects of character.

"While I was doing some work on my Sixth Step, a friend came by and brought me a present—an all-black coffee mug," said Ginny J. "There were some words written on the mug. They said, 'When the horse dies—get off.'"

The purpose of Step Six is to get off the dead horse—the negative character defects that stop our progress—and get ready to move on. In Steps Six and Seven, we have to lay it on the line about whether we are really willing to change or not. So these two steps are actually heavy-hitters. Why? Because all the probing self-exploration that we do in Steps Three, Four and Five builds to a climax in Steps Six and Seven where we are challenged to do something about it.

The main question now becomes: Do we truly have the willingness to turn loose these defects of character and absolutely believe that God can remove all these flaws from us? After the hard work of the first five steps, in the Sixth Step we come to a tranquil period of reflection. We look at our defects of character from several angles, and in different lights. We ponder why we are so attached to them, and why it is often difficult to let them go.

While it is an important step, working it is not that big a deal. All we are asked to do in this step is just what it says: Be "entirely ready," and then cooperate with God. But for some of us, it is not that simple.

"Those two words, 'entirely ready,' are the toughest words in the Big Book," said Molly N.

BECOMING ENTIRELY READY

Just how do we do that—become entirely ready? Who knows, you might even feel entirely ready right now. If so, fine: Go right to Step Seven. But if you haven't quite made up your mind about it, there are some things you can do that may help you to get ready.

The objectives of Step Six are:

1. To be fully conscious of our bad traits.
2. To become truly ready to let them go.
3. To keep faith that God can remove them.
4. To cooperate with God by doing our share of work.

Here is what we hope to gain from this step:

1. To get in tune with God's way of life.
2. To increase our faith in God's power.
3. To make some space so that God can act in our lives.
4. To believe that God can really do it for us.

No One-Shot Deal

"A lot of our character defects we are quite comfortable with," said Lynn C.

Because we are all human, and we like being comfortable, we will probably have to practice the Sixth Step again and again on all our personality flaws. It is an ongoing process. So the Sixth Step is not a one-time shot. In fact, in our continuing sobriety, we find that the Sixth and Seventh Steps become a part of us, and we continue this work on character flaws as long as it takes, as more is revealed to us.

"We bought a new house with a swimming pool," said Mike G. "My first time in the pool, I had to go to the bathroom, but the house seemed too far away. So I just let go in the pool. Then a thought hit me that was pure Sixth Step: 'It's the story of my whole life!' I thought. 'I am always peeing in my own pool.'"

Know the Enemy

There are only a few really major character defects, and most of them are mentioned in the Big Book in Chapter Five. You may be able to narrow down your list of imperfections if you go through your list, link up the defects which seem to be kin to each other, then find their Group Leader.

Obsession with Self is the mother from which all the self-off-shoots sprout: selfishness, self-centeredness, self-delusion, self-seeking, self-pity and self-anything-else. Dishonesty is a large umbrella covering lying, cheating, stealing, fraud and embezzlement, and lots of other petty offenses.

Fear is a monster defect under which all kinds of weird shortcomings hide. Look at your list and decide how many of your defects are fear-based. For example, behind every control freak usually lies some kind of fear. Find the real demon who is at the controls. Then you will have a better idea of what you are talking about when you say you are ready to have them removed.

Take Small Doses

Some of us emerge from our Fourth and Fifth Steps with a list of character defects as long as your arm. It is bewildering to consider so many. We don't know where to begin or how to cope with all of them at once.

One way to go about it is to take the Sixth Step in small doses. Just as we work our program of sobriety one day at a time, we tackle our defects of character one defect at a time. What you do is ask your sponsor to help you pinpoint the two or three most glaring character defects you have. You assign top priority to those, and put the rest of your defects on hold for a while.

"Work on being entirely ready to give up just these two or three," said sponsor Josh R. "Concentrate on just those, and pray about them for four weeks. Then go on to some more."

WHAT WE'RE GIVING UP

"I told my sponsor that one of my character defects was that I was too sensitive," said Deanna L. "'Are you really too sensitive,' she asked me, 'or are you just plain touchy?'"

Many character defects are defense mechanisms which have protected us and our self-esteem. When we are in the attack mode, we protect and build up our own self-image by unfriendly action against other people: criticizing, condemning, complaining, sarcasm, gossiping, character assassination, defiance—hostile put-downs, all of them.

"I wanted to be the boss—or I wanted to be the victim," said Amy.

Withdrawing from other people, physically and emotionally, is another passive, hostile act that puts us in a control position. We are defending ourselves by assuming the victim role, and are punishing people we love by giving them the silent treatment.

Back in Step One, we learned the difference between admitting, accepting and surrendering. Now, in Step Six, we begin the process of surrendering our defense mechanisms.

Getting High on Our Defects

"I have another addiction," said Ted S. "I am addicted to excitement."

In working our way through this step, we need to understand how much we love many of our character defects, how we cling to them, and how we get high on some of them. When the highs of alcohol and drugs are no longer in the value system of the recovered alcoholic and addict, some instinct within us learns to switch and substitute. Without realizing what we are doing, we find we can get almost as effective a rush from an all-stops-out emotional jag.

"I realized I can get high on anger," Ty O. said. "When I get really mad, the adrenaline starts pumping, the juices are flowing, I'm yelling, screaming and excited, and I have a blast. I feel I am really alive when I am angry."

To keep some excitement going in our lives, we may slide into a habit pattern of regularly falling in and out of love, accepting the pain of break-up as part of the highs and lows of the emotional orgy. Our disease inside us knows what to do to achieve a substitute high, and sets the wheels in motion.

"For the first couple of years I was an adrenaline junkie," said Katie N. "I got all hyped up and over-excited about everything, like being on speed. I drove people crazy. One day I got sick of being that way. I was really ready. I prayed hard about it and, sure enough, God removed it. My life is much more even now."

Gregory G. got his kicks from wheeling and dealing.

"I remember in one of the early meetings an old-timer said, 'There are no more big deals,' and I thought he just didn't understand life," said Gregory. "I thought, 'You old dingbat, there may be no big deals left in your life, but I am out there on the cutting edge. I am either having an orgasm or cutting a big deal.' Now, two years into sobriety, after working my Sixth and Seventh Steps, I understand what he meant. I am still on the cutting edge, but it is a lot looser out there now."

THE POWER IN STEP SIX

In working the Twelve Steps, we do a lot of admitting about ourselves. Now, in Step Six, we are actually making another admission: We admit we are entirely ready to risk opening ourselves up to God's power to change us.

The Power in Change

The power in Step Six has two faces to it. One side is the decision we make to let go of the harmful power we held. This was the power we used to control people, to hurt people with the destructive impact of our character defects. This was the power we possessed to terrorize ourselves with fear, or make ourselves feel like dirt.

The other side of the power coin is the deeper admission we make that we are willing to be changed—to pave the way for God to remove these destructive powers so that we can begin to live God's vision of life.

"I went to see my sponsor about a problem—just barged into his office," said Ted S. "It was the same old problem. It takes many forms. My sponsor threw his arms up in the air and said, 'Change it! Change it! I'm busy. Get out. Go change it.'"

"I went home, pissed off and insulted, pouted for two weeks, then said to myself, 'He's right. It's the same old pattern. My stuff is always the same old crap. It's just the details that change.' It forced me to do a mini-Fourth Step, look at the core issue, and take a Sixth and Seventh Step on it."

One definition of power in the dictionary is this: *Power: 1. Ability to act so as to produce some change.* In this meaning, power and action are linked with the aim of producing change. And that is the power-packed choice we make in Step Six.

"Change is an inside job," said Ross N.

True—many of the changes we go through in working the steps are inside changes, changes in the way we look at things and react to things. Then, when you start changing inside, things outside begin to change for you. And sometimes when we go through deep changes within ourselves, outside conditions can remain largely the same but we become happy and content within that framework.

"Change isn't what causes pain," said Rob S. "Resistance to change is what causes pain."

COOPERATING WITH GOD

There is a line in the TWELVE STEPS AND TWELVE TRA-DITIONS that says, in somewhat different words, that it is just plain dumb of us to think that God is going to do all this work for us without some cooperation on our part. We have to give God a helping hand if we really expect perfect results.

Adjusting Old Beliefs

"I don't have a drinking problem today," said Marie E. "What I have is an obsession of the mind problem. If I don't treat that, I will drink again."

Basically, what we do in working Step Six is to go through a process of attitude adjustment. "Attitude adjustment? You have got to be kidding!" you may say. No, really—what this means is that we learn how to let go of some old attitudes and develop some new ones to replace them. How come? The fact is, the dictionary defines an attitude as *a settled belief or manner of acting, a habitual mode of regarding anything*—in other words, a learned response that has become a habit.

Your character defects are attitudes. You character defects are habits. They have become deeply entrenched habits of behavior, just as drug addiction became a habit. Breaking some of them is as tough as breaking a drug habit.

"Just being sober does not mean being sane," said Debbie G. "The basis of every one of my character defects is fear. The fear turns into hurt and anger. But always behind the anger is fear. I turn it over, I take it back. Then my wheels fall off my wagon. They have fallen off a lot lately. I don't have a clue. God says, 'Have a taste of doing it your way, Debbie.' I don't know how not to be a bitch."

Each time we find ourselves hooking into a character defect, we try to do a displacement and substitute a Sixth Step attitude. In the back of our minds, we consciously carry around the thought, "I don't want this character defect in my life anymore. God, get ready to take it, please." Each time we become aware that we are actually into a destructive personality flaw, we learn to stop and say, "Okay, Partner, let's stop this games-playing. I am entirely ready to let go of this and give it to you." Or we just find the nearest mirror, look into it and say to ourselves, "We don't do that anymore, remember?"

An Exercise in Cooperation

"'Old stuff! Old stuff!'—that's what I have to keep saying out loud to myself when the old tapes start playing," said Diane S.

Try this exercise to learn how you can cooperate with God in becoming ready to let go of a character defect. These are actual examples of Sixth Step attitude adjustments that grew from D. J. C.'s Fourth and Fifth steps. This is what D. J. wrote and did to help displace her defects. As you read her lines, think about how you might work her technique on your own personality flaws.

Anger: I will keep my mouth shut. I will work a First, Second and Third step on the anger.

Willfulness: I will be more agreeable. I will let God and other people try it their way.

Controlling: I will practice "Live and let live" and the slogan: "I didn't cause it, I can't cure it, and I can't control it."

Write down three of your own defects and your cooperating actions. Put them where you can see them often. Or record them on a cassette and play them in your car. Sometimes this short prayer helps: *Do for me what I cannot do for myself. Help me to cooperate with you.*

Don't Be Too Hard on Yourself

"My sponsor told me to get up early every morning and stand naked in front of a mirror and say, 'I like myself,'" said Marilyn G.

Nowhere does it say that God is going to totally remove our healthy, natural-born instincts, appetites and sex drives. Our problem is simply that we compulsively practice them to excess. Drastic spiritual surgery is neither necessary nor desirable to remove our basic human desires. Instead, we become ready to have God bring them in line, within acceptable limits, so that we can enjoy them, enjoy ourselves, and enjoy others without causing damage.

"I think that's more of what it's about, if you read the Sixth and Seventh Steps," said Roland S., "it's about accepting yourself the way you are, and realizing you've got certain character flaws that might not ever entirely go away. There are things that caused trouble in my life when I was drinking that still cause trouble in my life today. But the thing is, I'm learning to accept me a little better. And when that happens, I accept you a little better."

Chapter Seven

CUTTING LOOSE

> *"Step Seven is where the*
> *rubber meets the road."*—Jessie T.

Seventh Step: Humbly asked Him to remove our short-comings.

"When I was working my Seventh Step," said Lucas H., "I asked God to remove all my shortcomings, especially the one about the wild sex fantasies I was always having. A couple of weeks later, one day I suddenly stopped smoking—boom! just like that. But the wild sex fantasies continued. I guess God has his own priorities about when to remove what."

The Seventh Step is the fish-or-cut-bait step. By now, we usually have reached the spiritual maturity to be willing to cut loose from our shortcomings—our personality flaws or character defects—and have God remove them. But willingness alone won't cut it. We need to ask for help. And in doing so, we put into action everything we have come to believe.

In working Step Seven, the action we take is very simple. We do what it tells us: We ask. How do we ask? Humbly, and in the form of prayer. In this step, humility is the key component.

"I had been humbly telling him to remove them instead of humbly asking him," said John A.

A Checklist on Readiness

When many of us completed steps One through Five, we discovered that the compulsion to drink and drug had been removed because we had been ready, entirely ready, and God took away the addiction. Can the same process work to remove our defects of character? In principle, the procedure is the same. Here are the highlights of what we should do:

1. Declare we are sick and tired of these flaws.
2. Admit we are powerless and that they make our lives unmanageable.
3. Believe that a Higher Power can lead us into healthful thinking
4. Humbly ask God in prayer to remove these shortcomings.
5. Really surrender these habits and feelings to our Higher Power.
6. Cooperate with God in every way we can.

If we faithfully do this work, here are the results we can expect:

1. To know that God is removing all our defects.
2. To finally say goodbye to old ways.
3. To be more considerate of other human beings.
4. To reject all compulsive belief systems.
5. To have the spiritual courage to live right.
6. To find ways to cooperate with God.
7. To see our imperfections being removed.
8. To begin to feel God's power within us.

"For God, it is so easy," said Angie C. "I kick and struggle and thrash around, and with God it's like a piece of silk. It just slips into place."

A Matter of Timing

How soon can we expect to get results? In the Twelve and Twelve, we are cautioned that we must go all out to ask God to remove our handicaps, but that we must be prepared to wait. And we may also have to be willing to accept less than perfection. This is called patience.

"My greatest character defect was impatience," said Ted S. "At six weeks of sobriety, I told my sponsor, 'My life is supposed to snap together—this ship is moving too slow for me.' That was seven sober years ago."

In working Step Seven, we get off to a good start, but removing all our flaws may actually turn out to be a lifetime process. Yet as we turn loose of our shortcomings and give them to God, our lives do begin to get better.

HOW WE HUMBLY ASK

Many of us have assumed we were humble, or pretended to be humble, when we were not. To go by the book, we need to get the feeling of humble. We need to actually become humble, and behave in a modest and reverent way, before we ask God to take away our shortcomings. It is a matter of common courtesy. Then we need to properly ask, and ask in a specific way.

There are socially acceptable ways of doing things that have become models of proper human behavior. If you want to approach the head of a foreign government, for example, you make contact through his ambassador. And you do it in a respectful, deferential manner. If you want to communicate with some person in Europe, you don't put a note in a bottle and throw it into the ocean. You ask for an AT&T overseas operator. When you want to make conscious contact with God, you don't send a FAX. You pray. That's the line of communication. If you don't know how to pray, you learn how to pray from someone who does know how.

The Humility Issue

Humility gets a bum rap in the world today. Both the term and the condition leave most people cold. Yet humility is the vital element in the Seventh Step. This step is often called "The Humility Step."

So it is important to know what these words mean—humble and humility. However, for an alcoholic or an addict, it may be easier to understand the meaning of humble by first looking at what it doesn't mean. In the dictionary, the words meaning the complete opposite of humble, called antonyms, are *arrogant, boastful, haughty, high, presuming, pretentious, proud*—a good character sketch of many addictive personalities. This is what we don't want to be any longer in approaching our Power Source.

Humble means *dependence, unpretending, submissive, deferential*—all gentle qualities. Don't confuse the two terms with humiliation, the bad word, which applies when someone bashes your self-respect, your self-worth, your self-esteem—humiliates you, often in front of others. Stay away from such people.

How can we become humble? First of all, we can stop being arrogant. We can stop being boastful. We can stop being haughty. We can stop pretending to be somebody or something we're not. We can stop acting high-handed, controlling, impertinent, smug, conceited and overly proud. These are things we can stop doing to become humble.

Positive actions we can take: We can depend on God's grace and power. We can be pliable, considerate, gracious, attentive and true. These are all very specific modes of conduct which, when practiced, can make us more humble. Becoming humble does not imply the begging attitude of a loser. It means the spiritually confident act of a recovered alcoholic-addict moving on with faith into contented sobriety and socially acceptable behavior.

How We Pray

You can pray standing up, sitting down, flying in a plane, driving a car, or getting down on your knees, a position highly recommended by most sponsors. Some alcoholics and addicts may find this latter posture embarrassing and uncomfortable, as they do a number of our A. A. customs.

"At the first meeting I went to where they all joined hands and said the Lord's Prayer," said Tracy T., "I thought, 'Oh, cripes, what'll they do next, Kum-ba-yah?'"

The kind of prayer we do in the Seventh Step is called Petitioning Prayer. That means you are petitioning, or asking for something. When you are a petitioner, your attitude should show respect. Westerners kneel. In the middle east, in the world of Islam, the reverent attitude is to kneel and touch the forehead to the ground. Hindus and Japanese Shintoists place their palms together and bow low. Timid alcoholics, afraid of being seen, lock the bathroom door and kneel on the hard tiles. That'll work. Others pretend they are searching for their socks under the bed. That'll work, too.

The Seventh Step Prayer on page 76 of the Big Book is a petitioning prayer, and most of us use it. But there are really no rules. If it makes you feel good to communicate informally with the God of your understanding, then say things like, *"Okay, God. I'm ready. Let's go. Remove them all, please."* Make up your own prayers and use them, whether on the go or on the knees.

THE POWER IN STEP SEVEN

"A lot of the power in the Seventh Step is in eradicating the negative powers that have such a hold on us," said Grita W.

The power in the Seventh Step comes from plugging into a familiar power that has saved our lives before. This is something we now know how to do. Once more, all we have to do is to ask. The power in the step comes as our courage to change boots up, and we make a commitment to cut ourselves free from our character defects.

For now we know that we have acquired the spiritual assurance to overcome our fear of authority figures enough to go one-on-one with God, to ask God to do something for us personally, and count on getting results. We find that much of the power is in becoming brave enough to give up the comfort we derive from many of our familiar old habits.

"'Well, hello old friend,' is how I greet fear," said Sheri F. "I am only comfortable when I am in fear and chaos. Under all my garbage is fear. When I am in fear I don't even know I am in fear. Now, I ask my Higher Power to remove my fear and replace my fear with love."

The Power in Seeing It Work

As we continue to work the step, we begin to get proof that God is answering our call when we see our shortcomings modified or removed.

"I had a breakthrough the other day on dishonesty," said Gregory G. "I ran a red light and a cop stopped me. 'Didn't you see the red light?' the cop asked me. Against all my instincts, I didn't lie. I told him, 'I saw the red light, but I didn't see you.' The cop had a sense of humor. He didn't give me a ticket."

When we realize "It really is working!" it gives us the power to keep asking. Even if the urge to drink flickers up in us once in a while, we know that God is always there to remove this Group Leader of all our shortcomings.

"I was fourteen months sober, and went to a business convention in another city," said Randall T. "There was a lot of drinking. During the big cocktail party, I prayed, 'God, help me Remove this craving to drink.'

"Then I went into the ballroom, and as I sat down at the long banquet table, I said to the old guy across from me, 'Sobriety is a bitch.'

"'You're not drinking? What are you doing about it?' he asked.

"'I'm in a program,' I told him.

"He reached into his pocket and tossed something across the table to me. I picked it up. It was a bronze, A. A. 34-year-anniversary sobriety chip. Man, I know there are no coincidences! That whole thing was a God thing."

Do Something Different

"I've made friends with my defects of character," said Dyana Y. "I can talk to them and say, 'Today I want to do something different.'"

Try a test run on the Seventh Step. Pick just one shortcoming. In morning prayer, humbly ask God to remove it. Then, as Dyana did, make friends with it. Whenever you feel it coming on, speak to it and say, "Oh, no, let's not do that now. God's working on that. I want to do something else instead." Then go ahead and do it.

"I cannot go out and mentally kill people, bury them, and then come to an A. A. meeting," said John A. "That means I have an emotional slip and I promised myself I would never do that again. If I stay there long enough I'll get drunk. I have to say, 'God, please remove this sickness from my soul.'"

Chapter Eight

USERS, HURTERS AND DUMPERS

"I lived to fight with people. That was what I did. People around me kept leaving. The nastiest four words I ever had to learn to say are, 'You might be right.'"
—Jeffry T.

Eighth Step: Made a list of all persons we had harmed, and became willing to make amends to them all.

"I went through people like they were Kleenex," said Kip K. "Whenever anybody said to me, 'Kip, I love you,' they were in big trouble. I was a people user, a people hurter and a people dumper. I had quite a list."

In Steps Eight and Nine we begin to clean up the mess we made while practicing our character defects. Becoming willing to do some fence-mending is the first move in our new human relations program. We begin the process of reconnecting with our fellow human beings, and we make a start at developing new people skills. Saying we are sorry is one of them.

Our destructive interpersonal relations were the cause of much harm to others and ourselves. While the ability to get along well with other people is not necessarily a God-given gift, it is a skill that can be acquired.

How do we begin to do this? First, we reflect on our sick emotions, on how many people we have deeply hurt, and how we hurt them. It is very important that we finally understand that it was our own alcoholic and addictive behavior that pushed others to their breaking point, triggered their anger, and brought out the worst in them.

What the Step Is About

There are five components we will study in Step Eight.

1. **Human relations.** We deal with our painful splits with other people and lay the groundwork for improving our skills in personal relations.

2. **People we harmed.** We try to recall other people we may have forgotten in our inventories, and we add them to our list of people we harmed.

3. **Definition and evaluation of harm.** We establish guidelines for judging harm, so we'll know whom we harmed and how we harmed them.

4. **Becoming willing.** We learn the secret of becoming willing, which is forgiveness, and that you don't have to like someone in order to forgive that person.

5. **The methods of forgiving.** Forgiveness is often the forgotten part of the Eighth Step. We learn how to forgive others and forgive ourselves.

What We Aim To Do

When you first read Steps Eight and Nine, it may seem as if we are doing this work to please other people and get them to like us again. Not true. We do these steps for ourselves. We tackle this job for a selfish purpose: to get us back on track. We become willing to mend the damage we caused, to unload remorse and disgrace, and learn how to get along better with others. Steps Eight and Nine are transition steps. They are power moves to dump guilt and shame, and to shape and redefine the new person we are becoming.

Our Messy Human Relations

Alcoholics and addicts have awesome records of poor human relations with other people in their lives. Personal relations are frequently disastrous with parents, brothers and sisters, friends, teachers, bosses, fellow workers, authority figures of every kind, and with lovers and marriage partners.

We did a lot of work in this area when we took inventory. Now we have to get ready to patch things up, heal the wounds, and learn the lesson: "I'd better not ever do *that* again!" The flip side of this is that the pain we have suffered in these old hurts will diminish as we overcome the blocks that kept us from making peace. We start to get right with people we harmed, and begin the process of improving our skills at handling people—a main thrust of the Eighth, Ninth and Tenth Steps.

MAKING THE LIST

"If your Eighth Step list is long," said Veronica J., "ask yourself if it is your own self-importance to think you could have drastically harmed so many people. Get real. Boil it down to the heavy-hitting names and go with them."

Maybe you could quickly list the people you ticked off on the back of an envelope. But most of us need to review our Fourth Step work to pull from it a list of people we really harmed. What's more, there may be other people we hurt whom we conveniently forgot to deal with in our Fourth Step.

Many times we leave off names because we figure these are the people who harmed us the most, not the people we harmed. Look at such cases: Are they nearly-forgotten episodes where we did something unacceptable, and the person struck back in fury? Their aggression is what we remember—not that we caused the situation in the first place.

When we pull together a list, we ask ourselves some questions. Are all the persons we harmed accounted for? Is the list filled with names which guilt rather than harm put there? In love affairs and sexual liaisons, we must understand that disturbed or destructive relationships have contributed to a lot of our anguish.

EVALUATING THE HARM

Although we may recognize that we did harm to someone, we may not always be so good at putting a name on that harm. This step helps us do that. We examine the various kinds of harm, the degrees and shadings of the damage we did to others. It gives us the information to know what we are apologizing for when we do our Ninth Step.

We need to ask ourselves: What constitutes harm? Does each name on the list pass the test—did we actually harm this person? If not, the name doesn't belong on the list.

The Twelve and Twelve defines harm as "the result of instincts in collision which cause physical, mental, emotional or spiritual damage to people." We might also add financial damage to the list.

The Primary Ways We Harmed People

If the way we treated people made them very angry and hateful, then we have harmed them. If our sexual behavior made people jealous, made them miserable, and made them respond with hostility, then we have harmed them. If we lied to them and manipulated them in ways to get money, we have harmed them. If we had relationships with people, then treated them indifferently and dumped them, we have harmed them.

The Work Plan in Part Two features seventeen questions you may ask yourself to judge whether or not you hurt someone. Evaluate each name on your list according to these yardsticks of harm.

BECOMING WILLING

"When we came to the Eighth Step, my sponsor told me that I had to become willing," said Rebecca J. "'I don't know if I can do that,' I said. 'Work on it,' my sponsor said. 'You'll just have to pray to become willing to become willing.'"

Here is where we begin to hit roadblocks. We find it is often very difficult to become willing to make amends. In cases where our offensive behavior infuriated people, they may have struck back at us in ways that really hurt us. So we have two-way hurt going on. That is what sticks in our minds now: how mean they were to us, and how much they hurt us—not what we did to harm them. Another roadblock can occur when we feel so guilty and ashamed of what we did that the idea of personally confronting this individual, actually having to apologize face-to-face, fills us with fear. We have a hard time forcing ourselves to consider making an amend.

We learn to become willing by praying. In prayer, we ask God to make us willing to make amends to all people we hurt. We say short simple prayers like, *"God, please make me willing to make amends."*

And then we learn to become willing by learning how to forgive. Forgiveness is the real key to becoming willing to make our amends.

Casey's Experience

"The first time I worked the Twelve Steps," said Casey F., "I did my Eighth and Ninth steps and made amends 'wherever possible.' On a couple of the amends, though I gave them my best shot, I always felt something was lacking. Something didn't click.

"Reworking the steps recently with my sponsor, I discovered what was left undone in my Eighth Step. The missing thing was forgiveness. I had become willing, but I hadn't forgiven. I had apologized and had made restitution where I owed money, but I had not let go of the bitterness and had not really forgiven them. I learned that even when you still feel anger, it is possible to apologize while keeping a hard heart toward the person you harmed. It doesn't come clean that way.

"I had to become willing to forgive myself, then forgive those people, before the amends would take hold. My sponsor put me through some forgiveness procedures. That did it for me. I went back to see two people, had another talk with them, and it was okay. They seemed forgiving—well, at least neutral, anyway—and we left each other with no hard feelings."

LEARNING TO FORGIVE

"It says in the Bible, 'Forgive us our trespasses as we forgive those who trespass against us,'" said Tiffany B. "And I thought: 'That means in equal measure, that God forgives me the way I forgive somebody who trespasses against me. And if I don't—God doesn't.' This tells me I'd better not mess with forgiveness, but do some big forgiving so I will be treated likewise."

If you go into a person's office or home to make amends, and your heart is still full of resentment, chances are your amends will fall flat. You may get kicked out. Why? Because people have good radar: the other person can sense that your words are false, that you don't really mean what you are saying. The whole purpose of our visit to make amends is to ask them to forgive us. And we haven't forgiven them first?—come on, get real.

"After a while I started to realize that if I wanted to have a sense of freedom, I had to forgive," said André T. "I began to realize that I had to release all the condemnation that I had for myself, for people I harmed, and for all the people I felt had harmed me. I had to take responsibility for my actions—what I had done to put myself in those positions."

Forgiving Yourself

Forgiving yourself is essentially a one-person show—only you can forgive you. But you can ask for help. First of all, you have to want to stop punishing yourself and want to forgive yourself. Next, you pray to your Higher Power to help you to forgive yourself. Finally, you accept your forgiveness and acknowledge it.

A short forgiveness prayer, which you might say at any time during the day or evening, might be phrased like this:

My Higher Power, please help me to forgive myself. Help me to be free of guilt.

You reinforce your prayers by accepting that they work and that God is helping you, and by supporting your prayers with positive affirmations which you say to yourself daily, such as:

I am completely and finally forgiven. It is all in the past and I am released from it. At last I am free to make my amends and get on with my life.

Forgiving Others

We may find ourselves holding back about forgiving someone because we know in our heart we don't like that person and doubt that we ever will. How can we forgive someone we hate? It may help you if you understand this: Nowhere is it written that you must like someone in order to forgive that person. In fact, you may despise some people and still be able to forgive them. You don't have to force yourself to like them—it wouldn't work if you tried.

Back in the chapter on the First Step, we learned the principle that feeling follows action. This is the same technique we use in forgiving someone. Whether we are one hundred percent willing or not, we go through the action of forgiving, and we trust that the feeling of forgiveness will follow. Winding up this chapter, there is a forgiveness formula that may work for you.

THE POWER IN STEP EIGHT

"How much power I gave away to other people! How much power I gave away to other things!" said Josh R. "The minute I give up and become willing, I get power again."

The persons we harmed took away our power. By hurting them, we gave them emotional power to influence us negatively. As long as we feel guilty, ashamed, and avoid them, they keep this power over us. They hold it until we make amends, free ourselves of them and neutralize their power.

The Power Push

Step Eight is a big step in getting your power back. The power we get is the power push we need to tackle and complete one of the most rugged tasks the Twelve Steps demand of us: to face in person once more each individual with whom we have had bad relations. It may seem hard, but as we become willing and forgiving, the power operates in mysterious ways as our Higher Power sets things up for us in directions we hadn't expected.

Charlotte's Experience

"When I did my Eighth Step and forgave myself and others, I became willing to make amends to an old friend I had fought with when I was drinking," said Charlotte T. "But we had both married and moved away from our home town, and I couldn't track her down. Last summer when I was home on a visit, I heard somebody call my name in the shopping mall, and there she was at the top of the escalator, waving at me, my lost friend, Elaine. We spent about two hours talking, and I made my amends. I learned that when we are truly willing, God seems to take over and arrange things. People appear when they are supposed to appear."

A Forgiveness Formula

In working the step so far, if you have decided that you have become willing to forgive them all, here is what you do.

Go where you can be alone and quiet, get comfortable, close your eyes and get calm. Think of how your Higher Power has helped you so far in your recovery, and believe that your Higher Power will help you now in the forgiveness process. Try to bring up an image of the person you want to forgive, and visualize that person sitting or standing opposite you. Then address that person by name, and say softly something of this kind:

_____ *(name)*_____, *I totally forgive you for all that stuff that went on between us. I forgive the entire thing. Where I am now, it's over. The resentment I held against you I now give to my Higher Power. I am free of it, and you are free of it. I wish nothing but the best for you, and I know you and I are both now in God's care. Let there be peace between us.*

When you are really willing, this treatment for forgiveness is a direct expression of your will clicking into God's will. As such, it is a powerful statement. You only need to do it once for each person on your list. To keep repeating it would diminish its power. There is a forgiveness ceremony in the Work Plan for this step in Part Two that may further help you to forgive.

Chapter Nine

REPAIRING THE DAMAGE

"Hug your demons or they'll reach around and
bite you in the butt."—Ted S.

Ninth Step: Made direct amends to such people, wherever possible, except when to do so would injure them or others.

"After I was sober a while, I found my wife sleeping with my sponsor," said Michael C. "I had abused her, neglected her, and was never there for her, so she turned to him for comfort. It almost killed me. I went crazy. But I didn't drink or drug. Later, we all three sat together in our home group while I told the group what had happened. We were all crying because we loved each other so much and it hurt so bad. Eventually we did our Eighth and Ninth Steps and forgave each other. We made our amends to one another and, though we are divorced now, we are at peace about it."

The central issue in the Ninth Step is the twisted interpersonal relationships typical of the alcoholic and addict, and how to rectify the damage we inflicted on others. Usually our resentments and pain are not dealt with until we do a Ninth Step. At the same time, the step teaches us a valuable skill we can use all our lives: How to fix problem situations between ourselves and others, and quickly get free of the pain.

Defining Amends and Restitution

The step calls for us to make amends and restitution. To *amend* means *to change for the better by removing faults, errors,*

94

or defects. The word *restitution* means *the act of restoring something that has been taken away or lost.* So in making amends, we are changing for the better, removing errors, and replacing them with something that was lost—like respect or friendship.

Emotional Blocks

Step Nine is not something we race into. We may be a year or more into our sobriety before we are ready to undertake this big step. And it is an open-ended step—we may be working it for the rest of our lives.

There are five obstacles or emotional blocks we have to overcome when first getting into the Ninth Step:

1. Confusion—not having a work plan to follow.
2. Fear—scared to confront the enemy.
3. Delaying tactics—putting it off.
4. Plunging ahead without much thought—being too hasty.
5. Being too proud—unwilling to humble ourselves.

To work the Ninth Step demands yet another deflation of the ego, and the spiritual courage to say, "I was wrong. I am sorry. Forgive me."

MAKING DIRECT AMENDS

Making amends to someone we have hurt can be an uphill battle within ourselves unless we have had a major change of attitude while working the first eight steps. The Big Book tells us the right attitude we should take in approaching the Ninth Step: that we should be "sensible, tactful, considerate and humble without being servile or scraping. As God's people, we stand on our feet; we don't crawl before anyone."

If we are still dragging our feet, we need to check out the emotional blocks listed above to see where we are hanging up, and perhaps do some more forgiveness work in our Eighth Step.

Making Amends to Yourself

However, not all of us left battlefields of broken hearts and bleeding civilians whom we shot down in our drinking and drugging days.

"I was a people pleaser and a total wimp as a drunk," said Paul R. "In Step Nine I strained mightily to come up with some dynamic damage I had done to someone—anyone. It wasn't there. My Ninth Step was a total bust."

One of the first things we do in Step Nine is to start being considerate of ourselves. When making our list of people we harmed, our own name should be high on the list. We make amends to our abused bodies, to our violated minds, and to our whipped spirits.

We make our amends to our body-mind-spirit by getting clean and sober and staying clean and sober. We make our amends by nurturing within us our increasingly intimate spiritual relationship with our Higher Power.

Making amends to yourself means restitution to yourself—restoring something that has been taken away or lost: your power and your self-esteem. In the Ninth Step, all this good stuff comes back to us when we thoroughly carry out the intent of this step.

PLOTTING A COURSE

Remember that in making amends to others you are doing Step Nine essentially for yourself and not for the persons you have harmed. You are the one who is cleaning up your act. You are the one who needs the healing and the lifting of the burden of anger and resentment, not the other person. If he or she also benefits from it—great. But this one is for you.

Setting Priorities

"I had done some shoplifting at Neiman-Marcus," said Marlo N. "During my Ninth Step, I called for an appointment and went to see the manager of the store. I told him what I had done, and the approximate amount of what I had lifted. I told him I was in

A. A., explained what I had to do and why my sobriety depended on it. Then I apologized to him, made my amends, and gave him a check in restitution.

"I almost flipped out when he picked up his phone, dialed the store intercom, and I heard him announce that all department managers should report to his office at once. He had them all come in and meet me, and treated me as if I was some sort of celebrity."

In getting ready to take the step, we set some priorities for amends-making. Get your sponsor's objective feedback on the names and situations on your list, and split the list into three categories. Title the lists:

a. The No Problem list—people I can make amends to now.
b. The Maybe list—people I may or may not make amends to.
c. The No Way list—people I will never make amends to.

This will get you going on your Ninth Step. You can make a beginning with the first group of names, the No Problem group, and possibly consider one or two from the Maybe list.

A FOUR-PART AMENDS PLAN

Here is an easy-to-understand, four-part approach to making amends to most people, one which has worked very well in many cases:

1. Write a letter of regret and apology to each.
2. Enclose a part-payment check if money is due.
3. Telephone those persons. If they live or work nearby, ask for an appointment to meet with them in person within a week.
4. Meet with them, and make your amends in person.

Writing a letter is a considerate opening move because it prepares them, and gives them a chance to digest what we're up to.

They'll be expecting our call. If we owe money, even a small check will show our serious intent.

Then we follow up with a personal telephone call asking them to name a specific time and place where we may meet with them. Don't ramble. Keep the conversation brief. Don't make your amends over the telephone.

Finally, we show up for a face-to-face talk. When it is a major amend and the person lives in another city, you may have to make a special trip. If the journey is impossible, your letter of amends may have to suffice.

After we make two or three amends, we feel more confident. By then, some names on the Maybe and the No Way list may seem more approachable.

What Do You Say?

Sometimes it helps to say a brief prayer just before you go in to an amends session. Here is one that has worked:

My Higher Power, please think my thoughts before me and speak my words before me as I go into this meeting. I trust you to help me.

You dress right—suited up or casual, as the other person will be dressed. You walk in, in a friendly but reserved manner. Don't offer your hand unless the other person does so first. Get right to the point. Explain that you are in A. A., and be open about your alcoholism and addictions being a major reason you are there. Don't get into spiritual matters on this visit.

Briefly recall the events which caused trouble between you two. Don't dwell on it. Don't blame. Don't argue. Say that in your program of recovery you cannot be comfortable about maintaining your sobriety until you have gone all out to make amends for your past behavior. Apologize for your role in causing the incident. Say that you forgive them, and that you ask their forgiveness, and hope your apology will be accepted. That's it. Then be quiet and follow the other person's lead.

Brandon's Letter of Amends

Here is an actual letter of amends written by Brandon S. to Sam O., a former sponsor and a good friend until Brandon moved to another city more than a thousand miles away.

> Dear Sam:
>
> I am writing to make amends to you for something I did a number of years ago. I telephoned you from Boston the autumn I was living there, and I was quite rude to you over the phone. I sensed I hurt your feelings at the time, and I was wrong both in willfully hurting you and in not clearing it up sooner than this.
>
> I hope things are OK for you, and that you are still sober and hitting the meetings at the club. I finish my MEA in Creative Writing at the university here in December and then, I guess, will go back home to live.
>
> Sincerely, Brandon S.

Note that the letter is brief and direct, and only five sentences long. Nothing more may be required than this. However, the nature of the wrong, the incident itself, and your feelings about it will determine the length of your letter.

When Money Is Owed

"I was walking with my sponsor in a mall," said Raul V., "and as we passed a fountain I said, 'I used to swipe coins out of that fountain when I was a teenager.' My sponsor said, 'That's stealing. You'll have to make amends.' I said, 'I don't believe this! How could I possibly do that?' He said, 'Easy. Every time you pass that fountain, throw in some coins.' I've thrown a lot of nickels and dimes into that fountain. I feel good every time I do it."

If you need to make restitution for money that was stolen or mishandled, figure it all out in advance before you see a person, and offer some kind of repayment plan. If you are unable to pay, be truthful about that, too. At the end of such a meeting, if an individual rejects your apology and rejects your plan—then that's his problem. You have completed your work.

Amends to Family and Friends

There are certain people to whom we may have already made amends by the change in our behavior toward them. These might include a lover or marriage partner, members of our families, or close friends. But some we may have treated quite badly, and we need to make proper amends to them.

Parents are often high on the amends list. If the relationship is harmful to you, get your sponsor's advice before making amends. But also consider that such a delay could be a cop-out to avoid making peace. When you grow enough in sobriety to see that there may be some possibility of repairing the damage that you and they have done to each other, by all means prepare to make amends. And give the same consideration to brothers and sisters from whom you may be alienated. Somebody needs to start it, and that is what this step is all about: repairing human relations.

It is amazing to hear in meetings how people, sober a few years, have made the first move for what turns out to be a loving reconciliation.

"I sat by my dad's bed in the hospital and held his hand as he was dying," said Chuck B. "He was an alcoholic who never made it into the program. Just before he died, he whispered to me, 'Take me to an A. A. meeting,' and a little while later he was gone. I did the next best thing. I put my five-year sobriety chip in his hand for his journey."

Amends in the World of Business

"When you arrive to make amends," said Randy B., "if you feel nervous, get back in the elevator, take from your wallet the little card with the serenity prayer printed on it. Study it, and talk to your Higher Power. Then take your Higher Power with you into the meeting. Walk up to the secretary and say, 'Tell Mr. Brown *we're* here.'"

Next in line after love relationships and family frictions, our places of employment are possibly the third big arena where amends need to be made. When it is a matter of bad tempers, bad judgment and disagreements, amends can often be made and accepted with satisfaction on both sides. But if manipulation of money is involved, it is a more serious matter. Restitution should be made. But sometimes full disclosure might implicate one or more people who might also be held responsible. These situations need careful thought and discreet handling.

WHEN AMENDS WOULD INJURE OTHERS

In making our amends, we do not in any case jeopardize or compromise other human beings. We must not implicate any other person, even though they were a partner in our negative behavior, sexual or financial. We may not mention their part in it without first obtaining their permission to do so. Even then, we think long and hard of what the possible consequences might be.

Lovers and Spouses

When we have been sexually active outside a committed relationship, we walk through a mine field when it comes to making amends. Sometimes a partner can withstand the cruel blow of a confession of infidelity, and the marriage or relationship will hold together. Sometimes it might not survive.

Guilt may drive us to confess. If we disclose all the details of our cheating, we may be hassled into revealing the name of the other person. It's disaster: We might destroy two people we love. The jealous partner or the jilted lover may seek revenge and strike out at everybody. Such blow-ups can end in separations, in divorce, and even damage the lives of children.

In situations where telling it all would cause this kind of harm to others, we back off—we don't do it. We may have to suffer our guilt in silence rather than cause further destruction.

Our Ex-es

In many instances, amends can be and should be made to former husbands, wives and ex-lovers. But we must first think it through. Could a letter or a telephone call from us trigger an outburst of suspicion and jealousy from their new mate? Or could seeing them again light up an old spark that could get us all into trouble? Do nothing that would cause more harm.

"After I made amends to my ex-wife, she asked me for a date," said Ralph L. "Her husband said it was okay. He trusted me. Wow!"

When It Might Cost a Job

When we have cheated or stolen from an employer, we may have to weigh telling all, revealing everything, against the knowledge that we may be fired. But what if there are other people who are dependent on us—spouses, lovers, kids? If we are out of work there may be no money coming in for rent, food, car or house payments, utilities, child-support payments and the like. Would our action harm these people and make them go without? Before making such amends, we need to talk over the situation, if we can, with those who may be harmed by our action. We should discuss the matter with a sponsor and pray for God's guidance.

When Amends Appear Not To Work

It occasionally happens that when we approach someone to make amends, they may have forgotten, and they may not know what we are talking about. So it was no big deal to them. On the other hand, someone else may have been waiting for just such an opportunity to blow us out of the water. They may blast us and shove us out the door without accepting our apology. In both situations the wind-up is the same: No matter what the outcome, you are doing this action for yourself, to get this monkey off your back forever.

So, actually, all amends work, if they are done for the right reason: to free us of the guilt and fear.

GETTING OUR POWER BACK

The major benefit of working the Ninth Step is that as we get straight with the people in our lives and become more and more at one with our Higher Power, our power is restored. A series of statements in the Big Book summarizes the restoration of power to the recovered individual who is in close touch with his or her Higher Power. This passage has come to be known as The Promises. It appears on page 83, at the end of the text on Step Nine.

The Power in Step Nine

In essence, what The Promises tell us is that if we have been thorough in working the steps up to this point, before we are even done with them we are going to realize these benefits:

We will experience a new sense of joy in life.
We will feel a new kind of independence.
We will no longer be afraid of people.
We will no longer be afraid of financial problems.
We will be at peace with the past.
We will no longer feel useless.
We will stop feeling self-pity.
We will become less selfish and self-centered.
We will stop being so self-seeking.
We will truly understand what serenity is.
We will develop a whole new perspective on our lives.
We will know how to let our new intuition guide us through
    things that once stymied us.
We will become more involved with others.

We will understand that our experience and strength can really help people.

We will know that God is doing for us the things we are unable to do for ourselves.

When we have made our amends, it is as though a great weight has been lifted from us. To virtually all of us who have worked the Twelve Steps, these promises have come true in our lives today.

Dyana Y.'s Ninth Step

"My bad relations with my mother-in-law, Helen, go back to the fifth grade," said Dyana Y. "Her son, Matt, was my friend. She did not want me associating with her son. She was social, and since I was a city girl who had come to their small town, she tagged me as white trash. She shamed me at every opportunity. In high school, Matt and I became involved. He was my first love. At seventeen, I ended the relationship, and went away to school. Matt was devastated. He took his frustration out on his mother.

"When I was twenty-two, I got involved with her son again. Matt and I got back together as a couple. Helen was beside herself. She was rude and hateful. I was two years sober—I got in the program when I was nineteen—and she would shame me because she knew I was involved in recovery. She attacked me one time and told me that I had this power over Matt, and that I was terrible for separating him from his family.

"Then Matt and I decided to get married. We planned every detail of our wedding and the reception—there would be no booze. And my mother-in-law-to-be was livid. She would start fights with us because we didn't want to have a party. She wanted to throw a party-party for us, but we and our guests were not drinking, and we knew it would be a party for her, not for us. Helen spoke to me only once on my wedding day—a catty remark.

"After the wedding, we made a big mistake. Matt's father

offered him a job running the family business. We went back to the small town and moved into a house they owned—no rent payments. Helen wanted to run our lives. She planned things. We declined. We saw them only on business occasions.

"One night Helen came out to the house when I was alone. She said, 'I think we need to talk.' She starts telling me all these resentments that she had. Then I lost it—I told her how she had hurt me through the years. She said I was a psycho, and started calling me names. Finally, I told her, 'I want you out of my life,' and I told her to get the hell out of the house. She did.

"For six months I did not see this woman. But it was eating me alive. I could not get this obsession out of my mind. One morning my counselor said, 'You need to go out there today and make amends.' I reluctantly agreed. I telephoned Helen first. I wanted to make my amends and get out fast. When she greeted me at the door, suddenly it was the first time I had not hated this woman in fifteen years. I told her that I didn't care who was right or who was wrong, I just didn't want to feel this hate anymore. I said I was willing to forgive myself, and forgive her, and I wanted to start over.

"She was thrilled. I wanted to go. But she wanted to talk and talk. I was angry again because I felt she had once more manipulated me into staying against my will. Back in my car, I screamed, 'Why, God, why?' Then in the silence, I heard God say, 'She needed to speak her piece.' I had a shift in my perception. 'Extend love,' is what I heard.

"And as I was able to extend love to her, everything immediately shifted. Now, since I'm not focusing on my mother-in-law, I will be able to see Matt more clearly. It has changed my whole relationship with my husband. I've released her. She's free. He's free. And I'm free."

Do a Trial Run

To try your hand at amends-making, select a recent case that is no big deal, an occasion where you were merely thoughtless or unintentionally rude but where you, nevertheless, hurt someone's feelings. Seek out that person and say, "I have a hunch that I hurt your feelings the other day when I said (repeat whatever you said). It was thoughtless of me. I didn't really mean to hurt your feelings. I apologize. Will you forgive me?"

Then see what happens. If this comes off well, then go for big game. Turn to Part Two and the Work Plan for Step Nine, and track down the people you really clobbered when you were drinking and using.

Chapter Ten

SCOPING OUT TROUBLE

"I have to take full responsibility for setting myself up. Every time I get shafted, I have to get into position first, right?"—Cliff C.

Tenth Step: Continued to take personal inventory and when we were wrong promptly admitted it.

"When things are not going my way, I leave the relationship," said Eric L. "I am there—but I am not there. I withdraw totally and isolate myself within the relationship. The only way out is to do a written Tenth Step."

The Tenth Step is an early warning signal that helps us to scope out trouble and defuse it before it becomes a major problem. Essentially, it is a continuation of the inventory process we learned in Step Four. The difference is that the self-appraisal we did in the Fourth Step was all based on *then*—the stuff going on in our lives when we were drinking and drugging. The Tenth Step inventory deals with *now*—catching new mistakes we might be making, and surveying issues in living which we encounter in sobriety.

The good news is that the promise of the Second Step has come true. A power greater than ourselves has restored us to sanity. So we become conscious of our first real miracle in the program—the compulsion to abuse alcohol and do drugs has been lifted. "We react sanely and normally," the Big Book tells us in the text on Step Ten, pages 84-86. "The problem has been removed." It points a direction for us: "Our next function is to grow in understanding and effectiveness."

THE POWER IN STEP TEN

"It's not about my drinking now," said Sylvia T., "it's about how I handle you, how I handle myself, and how I handle things."

When once again we are thinking sanely and healthfully, we are getting our power back. As we begin to function in harmony with people around us, we are getting our power back. Now, in Step Ten, we learn the power in practicing self-restraint. When we shoot off our mouths, or react angrily without thinking, we lose our power to be open-minded and unprejudiced.

"Anger turned me into somebody I wasn't supposed to be," said Jan C.

In the Tenth Step, the three main power points are:

1. Our developing instinct to sense a troublesome area before it becomes a major difference of opinion,
2. The insights and options that are revealed to us as a result of working the step, and
3. The peace it brings to our relationships with other human beings and with our God.

"One of the great things my sponsor taught me," said Grita W., "was this: 'You do not have to speak every thought that goes through your mind. You do not have to express every negative feeling that you have.'"

THE SORTS OF INVENTORIES

"It's about hurting people and learning not to hurt them anymore," said Teresa T.

There are three variations of a Tenth Step personal inventory that help us to sense trouble and nip it in the bud before it becomes a sore spot. While all personal inventories are essentially the same, they may vary in time frame and in the depth of the self-appraisal.

Three Classic Types

In the three versions of the Tenth Step inventory outlined below, we learn to develop the habit of self-analysis at three levels:

1. **In the radar-sweep or pulse-taking inventory**, done at any hour, we scope the field around us from time to time and mentally register: "What's happening? Am I doing okay? Or am I doing something wrong?"

2. **The daily inventory**, usually done at bedtime, is a think-through of what went on during our day. We mentally note what we did right, where we may have goofed up, and what we need to do in the morning to set it right.

3. **The half-yearly or yearly inventory** is a written account, a look back at our performance record to see where we showed improvement, where we were off track, and how we've grown spiritually.

When tackling this third kind of inventory, some of us like to get away to a weekend spiritual retreat where the atmosphere is right for quiet, deep self-assessment and meditation.

What To Look For

In all inventories, we must stay alert to spot resentments, fear, selfishness and dishonesty surfacing in us again. When these defects reappear to trouble us, we shift gear into some responses that we learned in earlier steps. We ask God to take away the defects. We talk things over promptly with our sponsors. We make amends right away. We work with others.

Then there are four other areas we need to address:

- We need to curb our emotions, control our tempers and mouths.

- We need to sincerely evaluate *all* aspects of each situation.
- We need to be ready to admit it when we are wrong.
- We need to be ready to forgive when the other person is wrong.

At all costs, we dodge being drawn into an argument. If we are hassled to argue, we fall back on the side-stepping, non-committing comeback: "You may be right." It will get you out of some tight situations.

THE FOCUSED TENTH STEP

A fourth variation of a Tenth Step inventory can be useful when a crisis occurs in our lives and we need to figure out what is taking place. This is called a Focused Tenth Step Inventory, focused on a particular situation.

Zeroing In on the Problem

The Focused Tenth is a technique developed to study the anatomy of a specific predicament we may be facing. It helps us to analyze it and understand our part in it. This kind of written inventory could be indicated when, for example, we may find ourselves in any of these circumstances:

- When a relationship is breaking up.
- When a marriage is heading for the rocks.
- When we have been fired from a job.
- When we have been offered a job in another city.
- When we are unhappy in our work.
- When something big happens that threatens us.

Such an inventory may be called for when anything makes us extremely angry, fills us with resentment, makes us start obsessing, makes us suffer pain, robs us of our income, or thrusts any sudden change upon us.

Problem Solving

The Focused Tenth Step can be an effective problem-solving tool. It can show us how to uncover our options, it can point to solutions, and lead us to consider lines of action.

What to do: Get plenty of writing materials, or a typewriter, word processor or a tape recorder. Tell the story of the event in full detail, as you would tell it to your closest friend. Leave nothing out. Then put it aside for several days or a week. Come back to it, read it or play it again, and attempt to analyze it. Go over the list of questions which follow, and write a paragraph on each one that applies to your predicament.

Getting Some Answers

In the problem-solving inventory, you interview yourself to find out what is going on. Make up your own questions based on the incident, or adapt the following ones to your crisis. Write, or record, your answers.

1. How do I keep setting myself up like this?
2. Have I done it before? When? Is it a pattern?
3. Do I set myself up for failure? How?
4. Was I to blame? Did I fail them? How?
5. How can I stop this craziness?
6. How was I a controller? How do I stop?
7. What is the honest name for what I did?
8. In this, what character defects are in operation?
9. Which character defects are top priorities?
10. Was I confronting, or non-confronting? How?
11. Did I "settle for peace at any price"?
12. Was I people-pleasing? How?
13. Was I conning people? How?
14. Do I make myself a victim? How?
15. How did I lack humility?
16. How did I hurt the others involved?
17. Where was I selfish and self-centered?

18. How was self-delusion part of the situation?
19. How is self-pity a factor?
20. How was self-seeking a major cause of trouble?
21. How was I being stubborn and childish?
22. How did I punish someone with my behavior?
23. Where did I shut people out?
24. What is my biggest resentment?
25. What is the biggest fear in all this?
26. What lesson can I learn from this experience?

After processing all you have written and discussing it with your sponsor, ask two final questions. Listen to your sponsor's input.

27. What are my options?
28. What actions should I take?

Try to write down five options, and from those select the actions to be taken. This is the bottom line to an effective Focused Tenth Step solution.

A RE-ENTRY POINT TO THE STEPS

"At work, I have this really great friend," said Molly N., "who is a bit of a hypochondriac. She got into a habit of saying to me each day, 'You look tired. Are you well?' or 'You look sad. Is anything wrong?'—things like that. One time I snapped at her and said, 'I wish you would stop laying this sickness number on me. I feel fine. Just lighten up, will you?'

"The minute I said it I could see her feelings were really hurt. She walked away and I went into a world-class guilt trip. I knew I had to do something about it, for her and for me. That night I did a Tenth Step inventory, prayed about it, and I did a Ninth Step amends the next day.

"'Marianne,' I said, 'I know I hurt your feelings and I am really deeply sorry. I didn't mean it, and didn't mean to sound so cranky. I really do apologize. Will you forgive me?' She did, and we hugged. But now when she sees me, she grins and says, 'I'm not asking you how you feel today!' And that's okay."

Working a Tenth Step often leads us back into the other steps. As Molly did, we may have to back up and do a Ninth Step to make amends. If the crisis is very difficult, we may reach even further back into the Twelve Steps for help. For example:

- If you feel powerless, go back and do a First.
- If it has you crazy, follow up with a Second.
- If you are obsessing, work a Third.
- If you need to blow off steam, do a Fifth.
- If you are ready to give up the behavior, do a Sixth.
- If you want the cause removed, do a Seventh.
- If you are willing to forgive and be forgiven, do an Eighth.
- If you are ready to heal the situation, do a Ninth.
- If you need more guidance, do an Eleventh.
- If you want to get your mind off the dilemma, do a Twelfth.

In the Eighth and Ninth Steps we are taught that, as we improve our skills in human relations, we may be working these steps throughout our lives. The Tenth Step is a springboard to launch you back into this process.

Carole's Tenth Step

"There had been a very bitter divorce the first year that I was sober," said Carole O. "One evening during a dinner party for some program friends, I got a phone call from my ex-husband, wanting to talk about our daughter. As I talked, my friends noticed that my facial expressions changed, my voice changed, my whole body posture changed. I was very hostile.

"Later they said, 'Carole, have you really dealt with this? Your whole body indicates that you have a lot of anger and a resentment at your ex-husband.' I thought I had hidden it pretty well, but it seemed I had not.

"'How do I handle it? How do I get in touch with this resentment?' I thought, 'What do I do?' Then my sponsor suggested a written Tenth Step. I said, 'How do I do a Tenth Step? I can't apologize to him, not knowing what to apologize for?' And she said, 'You use your Tenth Step the way you do your Fourth Step. Only let's focus on the relationship.' And suddenly it was very clear to me what I needed to do.

"So I started my Tenth Step inventory. And I started from the very first time I met my ex-husband and how the relationship had developed. What I discovered out of that inventory was that I had allowed myself to be abused emotionally from the very beginning of the relationship. Now I was able to see how I had set myself up, how I had determined how I was to be treated.

"Seeing that, I began to see how I could change. I went back and did a Fifth Step on it with my sponsor, I did a First, Second and Third Step on it, I did a Sixth and Seventh on it. Then I did Eight and Nine, to the point where I was eventually able to make amends to my ex-husband.

"I realized that he had done the very best he could with the tools he had. He was a good provider, and I had never thanked him for that. I realized also that if he had not been there to take care of me during my drinking, I would have dragged my child through a tremendous amount of hurt and pain. With this, I became very willing to make amends to him.

"Doing that Tenth Step allowed me to develop a new relationship with my ex-husband, one that is founded not only on forgiveness for the hurt that we both did to each other, but on self-forgiveness. It is one of not great friendship, but at least one of human being to human being. And we were able then to put our daughter's needs ahead of our own personal needs.

"The freedom that I derived from that Tenth Step allows me today to be able to target and focus in on those behaviors that I want to not have in my life anymore. And as God lets me remember them, I am able to do a Tenth Step on them. With that, I get a great amount of freedom, and the ability to change. And that is tremendous power that allows me now to live life the way I want to live life."

Tenth Step Readiness Test

You can easily take your own emotional temperature to test whether or not you are ready to take a Focused Tenth Step. Ask yourself the following question, and write down the answer to it:

What is going on in my life right now, sober, that is making me angry or unhappy, and is making me feel that I am powerless and losing control?

If you write down one or more answers, you are probably ready to do a Focused Tenth Step. If, for example, it turns out that what is bugging you is a relationship problem, you'll find help in Exercise 3 of the Work Plan for Step Ten in Part Two of this book.

Chapter Eleven

POWERING UP

"When I got to my Eleventh Step, my sponsor said to me, 'Hal, are you willing to give up a little bit of power for a whole lot of power?'"
—Hal N.

Eleventh Step: Sought through prayer and mediation to improve our conscious contact with God *as we understood Him*, praying only for knowledge of His will for us and the power to carry that out.

"I teach tennis to kids, but recently I had to play doubles with three real tennis pros," said Ted S. "I crumbled. I fell apart. I felt totally inadequate. Then, as we began to play, something clicked inside me and I started breathing in God and breathing out Self. It was a miracle, as though God became some part of me. When I did this, we won every game."

In the Third Step, we worked at breaking down the door that had been separating us from God. In the Eleventh Step, we take out the whole wall.

Ted's rush of power was a manifestation of "the power to carry that out." Ted clicked, hooked into God, and felt an immediate power surge that carried him over into winning. What happened to Ted was the embodiment in Ted of the empowerment that often comes as a result of working Step Eleven.

The step is about easy communication and a direct line of power between God and you. When we first read the words of the step, it may seem solemn. Actually, it is a big fat step, full of fantasy, mystery, and joy. It teaches us that God's power can become part of each of us, as it did with Ted.

"The power comes," said Garner P., "when you ask for it and when you need it."

IMPROVING OUR CONSCIOUS CONTACT

The step tells us to seek. It unrolls a spiritual treasure map and points out the trails we need to take: prayer and meditation. We seek—and we find. "He has come to all who have honestly sought Him," the Big Book tells us on page 57. "When we drew near to Him He disclosed Himself to us."

A Sharper Image

What we set out to do in the Eleventh Step is to build a more sensitive communications system between God and us. The aim is to improve our conscious contact, to send a clearer message to the Great Mother-Father Creator and receive back a sharper image of her love and his will for us.

"I carry around a spiritual umbilical cord, and I need to plug it in," said Daniel F.

Why so much emphasis on prayer in Step Eleven? It is because we must not get lazy in our spiritual development. Running just below the surface is the tendency to alcoholic thinking and alcoholic behavior, even while sober. We have been given a daily remission from our illness that is dependent on our spiritual health. To keep fit spiritually, we must connect with God frequently.

SEEKING THROUGH PRAYER

"In the beginning, I didn't know what to do," said Alan G. "My sponsor asked me if I had ever prayed. 'Sure,' I told him, 'I prayed for a Porsche and a million dollars, but nothing happened. Prayer doesn't work.'

"'You have not prayed, you have begged,' my sponsor said.

He asked me, 'Could prayer hurt?' and I said, 'No.' 'Could it help?' he asked. I said, 'Maybe.' 'Get on your knees and try it,' he ordered. I've been trying it ever since—and it's working."

While there are several recognized forms of prayer, once again the prayers we do in the Eleventh Step are of the kind called petitioning prayer involving a request or an appeal. During our day, there are several prayer intervals which the Big Book recommends. These form the structure of our spiritual communications system with God.

Evening Prayer

"I do a mental letter to God every day," said Angie C. "I pray, then I spend a few minutes meditating. It's not an either/or deal. Everybody talks about prayer and meditation as though it's one or the other, but it's not. It is part and parcel. It is talking to God, and listening."

In our evening contact with God, we get comfortable and meditate on the day just past. We ask ourselves questions, and ponder the answers:

- Were we mostly absorbed in ourselves and our own interests?
- Did we do something helpful for another person?
- When were we self-centered, mean, deceitful, fearful?
- Are we repressing or hiding anything that should be talked out?
- Should we make amends to someone?
- Where were we courteous, loving and caring?
- What did we do well?
- Where can we do better?

Then we wrap up this meditation with a prayer as suggested on page 86 in the Big Book: *God, I ask forgiveness for where I may have done wrong, and ask You to reveal to me what corrective measures should be taken.*

Morning Prayer

"One day I said to my sponsor, 'If I believe that God is within me, as you say,'" said Scott H., "'then when I am praying I am essentially talking to myself, right?' 'Right,' he said to me. 'You are talking to the God within you who *is* you.'"

The first thing we do on waking up is to pray. We might use this prayer, an adaptation from the Big Book text on page 86, or a variation on it:

God, direct my thinking, and let it be free of self-pity, dishonest or self-seeking motives.

We think about what is coming up in the day ahead. We reflect on what we hope to accomplish. We may wind up with a second prayer:

God, show me all through the day what my next step is to be. Give me whatever I need to take care of the problems that come up. Let me be free from self-will, and show me what I can do to help others.

Then we get ready to go out into the world with confidence, because we have tapped into God's power to get our brains working on a higher level.

A Problem-Solving Prayer

When we mull over the upcoming day, we may be undecided about what we should do in certain circumstances, and turn to another prayer.

God, I ask for inspiration, an intuitive thought or a decision.

Then we just let things happen. When we get into the habit of doing this every day, we are amazed at how often, as it says in The Promises, we will intuitively know how to handle a situation.

"If there are problems—for example, with my new boss—I

ask for a better idea," said Angie C. "I ask for an intuitive thought or a decision. I ask for the power to carry it out. I have lots of great ideas, and absolutely no ability to carry them out. But God is in that two-part business—the ideas and the power to carry them out."

An Any-Time-of-Day Prayer

When we feel uncertain about anything, there is another prayer we can slip into that may raise our comfort level:

God, I am no longer running the show. You are. Give me the right thought or the right action. Thy will be done.

We say the prayer at intervals until we feel better. If character defects are reasserting themselves, this prayer may help to minimize their effect on us.

Chrissie's Experience

"My sponsor told me to kneel beside my bed for ten minutes every night, to pray and to try to improve my conscious contact with God," said Chrissie G. "I did that, but I was uncomfortable, and nothing happened. Then one night I decided to get comfortable. I sort of sat on my heels, put my arms out on the bed, leaned forward and cradled my head on my arms, and just thought about God.

"I wasn't asleep, but I wandered into this sort of dreamlike state where I saw myself and felt myself actually kneeling at the feet of God with my arms and head cradled in his lap. He was stroking my hair. It felt safe and right."

SEEKING THROUGH MEDITATION

Though we may be somewhat more familiar with prayer, some of us are a bit leery about meditation. Maybe we think it is something mysterious or hard to do. It isn't like that. Very simply, meditation means being quiet and focusing on something. In this section, we examine different approaches to meditation. One of them may turn out to be right for you.

Transcendental Meditation

Because it is easy and effective, one form of meditation is widely practiced today. It is called Transcendental Meditation, or TM. The dictionary defines the term *transcendental* as meaning *beyond the limits of ordinary experience; super-rational, super-human, supernatural.* TM is taught in most larger cities and is quickly learned.

Following a brief spiritual ceremony, the student is given a mantra, often a two-syllable sound which is repeated silently, over and over, while meditating. A mantra is a sacred formula or incantation used in Hindu invocations, usually consisting of the name of some deity or a short address to it. The object is to focus on the mantra, to ignore all extraneous thoughts and sounds, and occasionally to transcend this world onto a super-natural plane. It is like asking the Spirit, "Let my mind merge with your mind for a while."

How To Do TM

You can begin to practice TM yourself this way: Use the mantra, *karim*, pronounced *kah-reem*, a true TM mantra. Sit upright in a chair, relaxed, with hands curled and resting on the thighs, and close your eyes. Plan to meditate for about twenty minutes at first.

Begin silently repeating the mantra. The mantra will find its own rhythm, often picking up the rhythm of the heartbeat or the breathing, in single or in double time. Remember that the mantra is not the end in itself. It is only a vehicle for getting somewhere. Don't expect to get there every time.

Roger's TM Experience

"I was meditating one night," said Roger R., "going with my mantra, and I got lost in the meditation. Time didn't exist. The mantra dwindled away, got fainter and fainter, and stopped. There was just silence. In a kind of detached way, I realized I had just been holding there for some time in what I call the white place, an empty space filled with white light. It was very comfortable and safe. I just hung in there and waited, wondering what was happening. Then I began to feel this kind of thrilling sensation, as though my skin was being lightly tickled. This feeling got stronger, like something radiating all over my body, until I was vibrating. Then it tapered off and left me.

"It was very emotional. I had never felt anything as wonderful as that. It wasn't sexual at all; yet it felt more like an orgasm of the mind. I didn't realize until much later that what I had had was a spiritual experience."

Centering Prayer

Centering Prayer is a spiritual format that binds prayer and meditation together. When combined, each gives power to the other. Centering Prayer is basically a contemporary renaming and repackaging of classic contemplative meditation as it is described on page 101 in TWELVE STEPS AND TWELVE TRADI-TIONS. Both methods derive from a very old spiritual formula developed in the fourth and fifth centuries by the Great Fathers of the Desert.

How To Do Centering Prayer

This early monastic form was practiced in four stages: *lectio, meditatio, oratio*, and *contemplatio*, roughly translated as reading, meditating, prayer and contemplation. Centering Prayer takes all of these, lifts them to higher spiritual levels, and unifies them into a seamless whole. The method works like this:

1. First you concentrate on the input—something you read, hear, or see—ingesting the spiritual message you are soaking up.

2. Then you meditate, which is repetition of the message many times, taking the message from the lips and the mind into the

heart and the gut, until something inside us says, "Yes. This is real. This is true."

3. Then you pray about what we have taken into our hearts and declared to be true. Prayer is us saying "This is so" to God, and communicating our love, our gratitude and our need.

4. Finally, you contemplate. Contemplation is a higher consciousness in which reading, prayer and meditation all become one. Our body and soul respond directly to God and say, "Yes!" We become prayer. We *are* prayer.

The book *Centering Prayer* will tell you more. But other meditation procedures can take you to the same place. Most libraries and spiritual book stores have many other good books on meditation.

GOD'S WILL FOR US

Because of our own willfulness, God's will for us and our will for us may often have seemed to be pointing in opposite directions. By improving our conscious contact with God, we try, as we practiced in Step Three, to bring the two wills into alignment until they become one and the same will.

God's Plan for Us

"I asked my sponsor, 'What do I do?'" said Chris P. "My sponsor said, 'What does God want you to do?'"

No one but you and your God can tell you what is God's will for you. It is a matter of becoming increasingly sensitive to the intuitions that begin to come to us from God. Still, some of us may have a fear of God's will for us. Substituting the words "God's plan for us" in place of the words "God's will for us" may lessen the fear. Everything in the universe seems to operate according to some plan, so there must be a plan for each one of us, right? For example, it seems reasonable to believe that we are now in a program of recovery because that was part of God's plan for us.

"I had to learn how to see miracles," said Lynn C. "I never

believed that they even happened, much less for me. I couldn't see them. I began to see that the things that were working in my life were outside of myself. I began to realize that the stuff I got into premeditated didn't work out very well. And the stuff that I was not even aware was happening around me turned out beautifully. Any miracle that you ever imagined, just pitch out; because the ones God has in store for you are fifty thousand times better."

THE POWER IN STEP ELEVEN

In the Eleventh Step, we have come to comprehend that we are, each of us, a child of God as we understand God. We accept our kinship with God. In seeking, finding and acknowledging God's power in us, we claim something that already belongs to us: our birthright that is in our genes, the gift from the Father to his children—our own God-given power.

The Power To Carry It Out

That promise in the Big Book on page 46 has come true for us: "We began to be possessed of a new sense of power and direction...." In seeking God, in improving our conscious contact, we have become empowered.

The term to *empower* means *to invest with power; to impart power; to authorize, to delegate authority to.* As we have come into our spiritual maturity, God has imparted to us the power to get our lives back together and keep them on track. But remember that we must claim the power. We must accept it.

On one hand, the power requires little effort on our part. It just flows in, and things begin to arrange themselves in our lives without our having to do much about it. We get an indication that the power is working in us when we realize how many times the right answer pops into our heads, or the right solution presents itself. Often a creative idea or conclusion will zing into our minds like a God-arrow straight from the source. We develop a heightened awareness of the seemingly strange coincidences that occur in our lives.

The power will surge in us in times of crisis, when some inner voice warns us in an instant to swerve to avoid a highway collision, or when we receive the strength to go through a severe personal loss and survive it.

The Power Crunch

"I asked for the power to carry that out—to get off my butt and to get into action. That's the power," said Grita W.

The power crunch is when the power is up and running, and we know what to do—but we walk away from it and don't use it. In the Sixth Step, we learned that one definition of power is this: *Power: 1. Ability to act so as to produce some change.* Power, action and change are tied together. Without taking action and changing something, the empowerment goes nowhere.

"I have to look at my own humanity, and at my role in acceptance," said Rob S. "I may ask for the power. I may be given the power. The power is there, okay? But I may negate the power, or I may simply refuse to accept it, or refuse to take responsibility for it. I have the power, but I must put the power into operation."

When the power crunch occurs, it is often fear that is jamming the transmission. It may be the alcoholic-addict's deep-seated aversion to change. It may be the fear of being held accountable for the task. It may be lack of trust in ourselves and lack of trust in God.

"I'm connected to the power supply, the power is channeled in," said Cliff C., "but it doesn't work unless I push the power button and tune in the channel. That's why I have to keep reminding myself, 'Turn on and tune in.'"

Signposts of Power

How can we know when we have reached this place? We ask ourselves, "How is the power making itself felt in my experience?" We search our feelings, our beliefs, and take a look at what is going on in our lives today. You may want to make up your own list of guiding signs as you encounter them, but here are some road markers which have helped many of us to recognize that God's power has come into us:

- We have a heartfelt feeling of gratitude.
- We have a sense of finally belonging.
- We have a belief we are being guided.
- We have an overall feeling of well-being.
- We feel we are being nurtured and cared for.
- We are experiencing the joy of living.
- We have a deeper conviction of our own worthiness.
- We are competent and confident.
- We feel needed and wanted.
- Good things are happening for us.
- We can sense the power now within us.
- We are able to take action on issues in our lives.

Nevertheless, we must always remember that the handing down of authority and power is conditional. It depends upon our continuing spiritual progress. Our power is entrusted to us—it can be revoked at any time. God still retains the ultimate power. Our power can fade away if we blow the whole thing and betray the trust.

How the Power Came to Larry

"I was about nineteen months clean and sober, working in an ad agency as a copywriter, when I first became aware of the power," said Larry E. "One day I spent hours trying to write an ad. Nothing worked. To deal with the frustration, I shut the door, closed my eyes, relaxed, centered myself, and began meditating. After maybe fifteen minutes I began to write again.

"It was as though a switch had been flicked on. Later, thinking about it, it seemed as if the words streamed down through the top of my head into my fingers and onto the keyboard. The ad wrote itself. I had nothing to do with it. It was as if God were saying, "See, Larry, when we do it together, how really easy it is?"

A Power Imagery Meditation

Here is a simple exercise in meditating which you may find easy to do. Sit, relax, and close your eyes. In your creative mind, see yourself standing in front of the door mentioned in Step Three, the door that had been separating you from God. You are inside yourself, but you are outside yourself, too, observing what is going on. Reach out your hand, touch the door, and imagine your hand and arm passing right through the door, as if in a science fantasy or space opera. Pull your arm back. Then, very slowly, step forward and watch your body walk into the door, merge with the door, move through the door and disappear beyond. The you inside you is now on the other side of the door. You are in a different place. What do you see there?

Chapter Twelve

REACHING OUT

"God gives you the power, but you need to put God's purpose up front."—Kenneth Copeland

Twelfth Step: Having had a spiritual awakening as the result of these steps, we tried to carry this message to alcoholics and addicts and to practice these principles in all our affairs.

"Though I had been sober two years, I was a compulsive organizer and controller," said Ginny J. "I had my kids, my husband and my house looking like pictures in a Bloomingdale's catalog. We looked as though we were all for sale. I wanted to stop doing this.

"I was working the steps again, and one night, unable to sleep, I went out on our patio around two in the morning. I looked up at the sky, at the stars and the moon. 'God,' I said, 'everything in your universe seems to work in perfect order and harmony. Do you think you could do me?' And then I said an Eleventh Step prayer. In the morning when I woke up, I felt something was different. Something had changed. I felt on track. Within a short time I began working with others and sponsoring several women. I know now that my spiritual awakening came that night on the patio."

An inward journey has been our course in the first eleven steps—getting well, discovering who we are and why we behave the way we do, forming a partnership with our Higher Power, and recognizing our empowerment by God. Now, the Twelfth

Step becomes a celebration of life as we turn outward, redirecting our focus from ourselves onto others.

THE POWER IN STEP TWELVE

"Where there had been a trickle, there now was a river which led to sure power and safe guidance from God...." This declaration in the chapter on Step Twelve in TWELVE STEPS AND TWELVE TRADITIONS salutes a high point in our spiritual development. Sure power and safe guidance are what we have worked for. By this time, having experienced the delegation of power into us, we are ready to begin giving away some of the power that has come to us through God's grace.

The Power Lift-Off

An important thrust of the power payoff in this step is that it takes us outside ourselves. The step is like a mother bird pushing the fledgling sparrow out of the nest and saying, "Okay, you have learned everything I had to teach you. Now go out into the world, flap your wings around a little, and then begin practicing the things I taught you."

The payoff comes to us in three ways:

1. The life-altering power of the spiritual awakening which shifts our attitudes and actions. It is the change that sets everything else in motion.

2. The thrill of discovering that working with other alcoholics and addicts has the power to make us forget about ourselves and our own issues.

3. The relief that comes as we learn to practice the principles of the program to solve problems, enrich our lives, and lighten up a little.

"When I learned to laugh at myself, I found I have a constant source of entertainment," said Jessie T.

THE SPIRITUAL AWAKENING

In Twelve Step talk, we speak of two varieties of spiritual happenings. One is the spiritual awakening. In most cases, the awakening evolves slowly over a period of time. The other occurrence is the spiritual experience, which can come over us rather suddenly, and can be of a more dramatic nature. Whether our spiritual perception happens slowly or in a sudden moment, it usually results in a major transformation in our personalities and the way we look at things.

Terry's Awakening

"I thought I had done the Eleventh Step," said Terry F. "I had taken a course in meditation, I had read metaphysical books, and I had talked a lot about God in meetings. I had done all the outer things. But finally I realized it was all head stuff. What I hadn't done was to seek God in my heart.

"A new sponsor had told me, 'What you are looking for is already there.' I didn't understand at first. On a trip to New York, one afternoon I walked into St. Patrick's Cathedral, though I am not a Catholic. The church was quiet, almost empty. I knelt at the altar steps. After a while I said, 'Help me. Show me how.'" I waited, just hoping for some message. Then a great feeling of peace poured into me. It filled me. It was so sweet. It stayed with me for a time, then it diminished to a gentle tranquillity. I hated to leave.

"I know now that God was with me all that time. I had just never asked him to help me make contact. But he helped me. He was there. That was my spiritual awakening."

When Does It Occur?

The opening words of the step, "Having had," assume that the spiritual awakening has already happened. "Whoa!" some of us may say. "Just when did this take place? Did I miss something?" Some will argue that it occurs during the Twelfth Step because that is where it is mentioned. Others may insist that, no, "having had" is past tense, so it properly takes place in or around the Eleventh Step as a result of prayer and meditation. The answer is, of course, that the spiritual awakening can happen at any time.

"I think if you did all eleven steps, you had a spiritual experience," said Brian S. "You don't need to sit around and think about did you or didn't you. Just don't worry about it—you did. You'll find out later that you did, and didn't even know it. That's a very important thing to think about."

Carlos' Spiritual Experience

"One night I knelt by my bed," said Carlos M., "and, on impulse, I decided to try purely non-verbal communication with God. I emptied my mind and got still. For the longest time I knelt there, feeling love, just yearning without words to make contact. In spite of my intentions, some real words drifted across my mind: 'I seek the One known as God the Father.'

"Within seconds, a tingling sensation started at the top of my scalp and slowly spread down over my neck, my shoulders and my body. It was like a faint low-voltage electrical current. It got stronger. After a while it toned down and pulled back a little. When it was gone I was crying, and I had a feeling of pure joy. I knew I had felt The Presence."

Marty's Spiritual Experience

"I had to have a spiritual experience or I was going to die," said Marty G. "Drugs and alcohol gave me a sense of power, that I was important. At the cap and gown ceremony at school, I was on mescaline and started hallucinating badly. I came unglued. They carted me off to treatment. After a while at the clinic, one day my image in the bathroom mirror disappeared and what I saw was a light. I saw it as the Holy Spirit.

"I began to tingle all over. I began to sob. I knew God, and I knew God had always been there for me. And I knew I didn't have to earn God's love. For weeks I saw everything like a child.

My spiritual experience didn't come through meetings, but it is sustained through meetings."

CARRYING THE MESSAGE

For people like ourselves, the best prescription for staying sober, clean and sane is always the same: get busy working with other alcoholics and addicts. There is a deep sense of satisfaction in helping people get sober, seeing them become more open, begin to share with others and begin to make a connection with a Higher Power. "This is an experience you must not miss," says the Big Book.

Spending Our Power

In this way, we learn the core message of Step Twelve: It is about being there for somebody. It is about giving back, about caring enough about other scared confused people to pass on to them the wisdom we have learned in our recovery. In doing this, we become part of the loop, carrying the healing principles of the program and handing them on to those who follow us in recovery.

We have reached a place where we are rich enough in our sobriety to begin spending our power, giving it freely to those who need it. And as we spend it, we find that our power is replenished.

Sylvia on Service Work

"It makes me angry when I see people sit there and say they're grateful for sobriety and that they enjoy life—and there is no inflection in their voice and no action in their program," said Sylvia T. "No action! I was taught that gratitude is action.

"As long as I can sit there in a meeting and say, 'I'm grateful for my sobriety,' I have to also say, 'Well that's really nice, Sylvia, but where is the action, where is the service work, where are the people that you're working with, the new people? Why are you not going to detox units? Where's the gratitude? You sit here and you look good, but there's no action.'

"I've learned how to say instead, 'Yes, I'm glad for sobriety—now what can I do?' If I don't get out of myself, and if I don't at least try to help somebody—and I have bungled many times, I have made stupid remarks and done stupid things in the line of service work, but at least I do it—I've got to do all that to stay sober. Because I have been told that as long as you're doing service work you're not going to get drunk.

"I find that today my life is so much better if I can take that attitude of gratitude, and then take the action that goes with it. It doesn't take that much energy. Sometimes it takes a few hours and a tank of gas. And sometimes it's just forty cents for a cup of coffee for a newcomer, and sitting there with him or her for twenty minutes. I can't hold on to it if I keep it to myself. That is not the way my life grows today."

How To Talk with a Newcomer

"The Twelfth Step helps you be a benefit," said Brian S. "If you don't get to a point where you think that you need to give some of this away, and do something for what's been given to you, I think you're in a lot of trouble."

Young newcomers need to connect right away with some young people of their own age group with whom they can identify, young program people who know where they are coming from. In our eagerness to help, the biggest mistake we can make with newcomers is to speak a non-stop monologue, trying to talk them sober in one session. Give them a break; just be a friend. First, just introduce yourself and talk generally, anything that comes easily. Try to bring the talk around to some incident involving alcohol and drugs. Then let the newcomer know something about yourself, your various addictions, your lack of control, the trouble you got into. Try to draw them out and get them talking about their own problems.

If they seem to be in a depression, tell them what alcohol and drugs did to you. If they loosen up a bit, hit on a few funny scenes you got into. Ask if they can identify with those, and try to get them to tell you about some of their wild trips. Tell them how slow you were to catch on that you were really sick. Let them know about the times you tried to stop and found you couldn't. Explain to them the deal about it's the first drink that gets you drunk—how with you it always led to a second, third, and on to a big drunk or drug scene. If they open up, briefly explain the Twelve Step program. Describe the Fellowship and the sharing in meetings. Give them a meetings' schedule. Get them a copy of the Big Book. Give them your telephone number and invite them to call. Get their telephone number. Take them into a meeting. If they don't call you, call them. Ask if there is anything more you can do.

Anywhere during the conversation, if it becomes plain that they really are not ready to quit, back off. It is a waste of your time to try to convince them or rescue them. Your time is better spent helping those who want help.

More Tips on What To Say

Here is a checklist of more things you may want to consider, and things you might want to avoid, in working with new persons:

- Do keep in mind that they are sick.
- Do ask if they are willing to go to any length to quit.
- Don't preach, don't teach.
- Don't dive into the Big Book right away.
- Don't suggest that they are alcoholic or addicted.
- Don't scare them by talking religion.
- Do touch on spiritual principles.
- Do tell them alcoholism is a fatal disease.
- Do condense your story. Don't ramble.
- Do try to get them to reveal how they are feeling.
- Do speak in the kind of language they talk.
- Don't get into heavy theological or metaphysical concepts.

- Do say they need not buy your idea of God.
- Do ask if they can believe in some power greater than themselves.
- Don't offer advice on personal matters.
- Do make a date to meet at another meeting.
- Don't go to bed with a newcomer. They're too vulnerable. Getting into something heavy could wreck their fragile sobriety. You'd be almost as vulnerable yourself. It's a complication you don't need.

Twelve Ways To Do Twelfth Step Work

The Twelfth Step talk with a newcomer is only one of the ways in which we help carry the message. Anyone who is serious about doing service work has a great choice of ways to offer help. Among them:

- Making coffee before meetings.
- Cleaning up after meetings.
- Sharing in beginners' meetings.
- Serving as a host or greeter before meetings.
- Serving as group secretary or treasurer.
- Chairing or leading meetings.
- Taking meetings to treatment centers.
- Taking meetings to detox units and halfway houses.
- Speaking at speaker meetings.
- Volunteering for A. A. telephone duty at night and weekends.
- Being a temporary sponsor to a newcomer. Sponsoring someone is probably the most satisfying form of Twelfth Step work you can do.

PRACTICING THESE PRINCIPLES

What, exactly, is a principle? The dictionary tells us that a principle is *a general truth or proposition, a settled law or rule of action, especially of right action.* By this definition, the Twelve

Steps are definitely principles themselves—as are other principles that are revealed as we study each step.

Living the Principles

"It's a beautiful view when you step over yourself," said Deanna L.

Self-examination, calling for changing old belief systems and actions, is a major principle of most of the steps. The principle of honesty, especially self-honesty, figures prominently in ten of the steps. Other cornerstones of the program are hope, faith, humility, courage, open-mindedness, willingness, forgiveness, serenity and service to others. Reliance on a Higher Power, or God-consciousness, is the glue that holds all the steps together.

The destruction of ego—of selfishness and self-centeredness—is a vital ethic dealt with in the majority of the steps. It reaches its peak in Step Twelve as we become others-conscious rather than self-conscious.

Problems in living don't stop just because we are clean and sober. Let's look at three cases, problems faced by people in recovery, and study how they practiced the principles of the steps to solve their difficulties.

In Bondage to a Parent

"When I was sober five years, I lost my job and was out of work quite a while," said Glenn C. "I finally went to my father for help. My dad is a practicing alcoholic and a rage addict who dominated me, verbally abused me and shamed me. When I asked for his help, he raged and rejected me again.

"I turned to the Big Book and found myself rereading the story on 'Freedom from Bondage' on page 544, about the woman in bondage to a resentment against her mother. So I did a written Tenth Step on bondage and resentment, and then I worked the steps again to pray for my father and for freedom from bondage to him. I started with the First Step, like this: 'I admit I am powerless over this resentment and bondage to my father.' I reworked all the steps around freedom from bondage, resentment, and shame.

"I also said the Third Step prayer on 'bondage of self' and the Seventh Step prayer. This time I did the forgiveness part of the Eighth Step. And a strange thing happened. I was enabled to see him clearly as he really is: another tortured alcoholic, and I was able to feel compassion for him.

"As a result of doing the steps on this relationship, God put another idea in my head. I began going to Al-Anon meetings and learned how to lovingly detach from the drunk in my life—my father. Now I am free of bondage to him, but in a way I hadn't expected."

Addiction to a Person

"I was in a relationship that had incredible highs and lows," said Marcia T. "We would destroy each other, split up, get back together again, and now we were split up once more. One day, my sponsor, without actually telling me so, somehow led me to question whether I was actually addicted to Carl the same way I was addicted to alcohol, speed and cocaine.

"I went to some Sex Addicts and Love Addicts Anonymous meetings, but felt more comfortable in my A. A. meetings. Finally I decided, with my sponsor's help, to work the Twelve Steps again on this new addiction—addiction to a person. I started with a Tenth Step inventory on my relationship with Carl, did a Fifth with my sponsor, and went back and started with Step One: 'God, I admit I am powerless over this addiction, my obsession with Carl—that my life has become unmanageable because of it.'

"It took quite a while, but the pain gradually lessened. It was not easy. I had a few emotional relapses into self-pity, but I kept at it and prayed a lot. I continued with a daily Tenth Step, writing in my journal how I felt about it.

"I have grown comfortable living just with myself. I never thought I could live without somebody to fix me. I am not ready yet to do a real Ninth Step amends, but I have faith that, when I am ready, God will point the way."

Practicing the Third Step in Bed

"I felt my marriage was in big trouble," said Lisa M. "Bart, my husband, had withdrawn from me and there was very little communication between us. My sponsor had me do a written Tenth Step on the marriage, then she had me work most of the steps over again, centered on the marriage. She made me write my own versions of each step in the form of a prayer. She suggested daily meditation and prayer on this, which I did over many months.

"I did a lot of Third Step self-examination on my selfishness, self-centeredness and control issues. I admitted the exact nature of my wrongs to myself, and did a Fifth Step, admitting them to her. I meditated about it, and prayed, sharing it with God.

"My Sixth and Seventh steps went like this: 'God, I am entirely ready to have you remove all my defects of character—my controlling, my bossiness and my critical attitude—all the things that are causing trouble in my marriage.' 'I humbly ask you, God, to remove these problems from me and from Bart, to take them, release us from them and restore our comfort and our communication with each other.'

"Bart and I did a Ninth Step jointly, forgiving each other and making amends to each other. Then we talked together at length, sharing our feelings.

"The marriage is back on track, and the sex is great now. I learned that really practicing the Third Step in bed was great sex therapy—forgetting about selfishness, self-centeredness, self-seeking, and giving full attention to my partner's needs and wants. Bart smiles a lot now."

Test Your Giving-Power

You can do a simple experiment tonight to test your giving-power. Go to a meeting and get there early. Spot one or two newcomers—by now you know that look. Go up to them. Talk with them. Get them talking. Sit beside them in the meeting. After the meeting, take them with you for coffee or a burger. Tell them your story. Encourage them to tell you theirs.

Within that short span of time, you can be practicing many of the principles of this program, and fulfilling our primary purpose: to stay sober ourselves and help others to achieve sobriety.

How will you feel afterward? The highs you can get from sharing your power in this way can lift you up and sustain you for a lifetime, as long as you continue to do it.

"The first nine steps are ways to learn to use God," said Lynn C. "I learned that Steps Ten and Eleven are ways you become closer to your God. And I learned that Step Twelve is where God uses you."

PART TWO

A Twelve Steps Workshop

"The reason you should try the Twelve Steps is that your way stinks. You are the product of your whole game plan for living."—Randy B.

"They tell you, 'All you have to do is go to meetings, don't drink, and read the Big Book.' What they really mean is, 'All you have to do is go to meetings, don't drink, read the Big Book——and change your whole freaking life!'"—Tommy P.

HOW TO WORK THE STEPS

"I hate to write," said Susan L. "I force myself, even when I can only begin, 'This sucks, this sucks.' But there is nothing that will show me what I'm thinking like writing it all down. I call it 'Taking out the trash.'"

Writing things down is a widely accepted part of working the steps.

"On every step, my sponsor had a set of questions to which I had to write out the answers," said George C.

It is easy just to read the steps and say, "Okay, I can understand that, I can do that." Then we think we have done the steps by ourselves in our heads but, later, we may never be quite sure whether we have actually taken the steps or not.

"There is something that begins to happen when I write about something that is bothering me," said Debbie D.

What happens, when we start to write, is that the thing that is bothering us is no longer just in our heads. We see it, in black and white, in front of our eyes. It confronts us. Writing it out helps us to get honest with ourselves.

"I found out a lot about myself that came out of that pencil— stuff that would never have come out of my mouth," said Jack G.

Many sponsors were interviewed for this section, and they contributed their ideas to the Work Plans. When you choose to study these reading assignments, complete the writing exercises on each step, and then take the step with a sponsor as suggested, you can be sure that you have worked each one of the Twelve Steps.

If reading is a problem, you can get the books, ALCOHOLICS ANONYMOUS, TWELVE STEPS AND TWELVE TRADITIONS, and NARCOTICS ANONYMOUS as audio-cassette tape albums——talking books on tape. You can study by listening. In most cities, your local A. A. Intergroup Office may have the A. A. tapes. Big Book, 7 tapes, $35.25; Twelve and Twelve, 5 tapes, $35.25. The Narcotics Anonymous basic text, a three-tape album, $8.00, can be ordered from World Service Office, P.O. Box 9999, Van Nuys, CA 91409. Or by phone: 818-780-3951.

If writing is a problem, you can speak the writing exercises into a small tape recorder and play back the tapes for your sponsor.

Many attend step meetings and participate in step study semi-nars. These are excellent preparation, providing you go beyond the discussion stage and actually do the work. That is what they mean when they say, "Work the steps and work your program."

1

First Step:
We admitted we were powerless over alcohol and drugs—
that our lives had become unmanageable.

WORK PLAN FOR STEP ONE

What to read and study. In ALCOHOLICS ANONYMOUS, read pages xiii-43 and pages 58-60. In TWELVE STEPS AND TWELVE TRADITIONS, read pages 15-24. If you are addicted to drugs, in NARCOTICS ANONYMOUS read pages 19-22. Read some of the personal stories.

Meet with your sponsor. Read aloud with your sponsor some passages from the books. Discuss what you have read and ask any questions on your mind.

Personalize the step. Make it yours: "I admit I am powerless over alcohol and drugs—-that my life has become unmanageable." Put whatever words you need in it to make it work for you.

Exercise 1. Write about hitting bottom. Get a large, wirebound notebook. Title a page, "Hitting Bottom." Write about what brought you into recovery.

Exercise 2. Write about being powerless. Title a page "I Am Powerless Over...." List all chemical substances over which you are powerless. Then write about the times when you were out of control and what happened.

Exercise 3. Write about your unmanageable life.

1. List the ways in which your life had become unmanageable.
2. List things you have lost because of alcohol and drugs.
3. List relationships that split up because of drinking and using.
4. List the ways in which your life seems unmanageable today.

Take the step with your sponsor. Meet personally with your sponsor and take the step by reading aloud all you have written. Discuss it.

A closure to the First Step. If you and your sponsor are agreeable to the idea, choose a quiet place with a good feeling where you won't be interrupted. Get close. Sit facing each other, and reach out and take your sponsor's hand. Make up your own words, or use the following dialogue as a guide. Talk it, if you can, or read it.

Sponsee: *You are my sponsor, and I want to formally take the First Step of the Twelve Steps with you, and ask you to witness it. I tell you, from my heart, that I admit I am powerless over alcohol and drugs, and that my life has become unmanageable. Will you witness my taking the First Step?*

Sponsor: *I will, and I do witness your First Step. I heard it. It is done. Remember it each day, one day at a time.*

Sponsee: *Thank you for witnessing my First Step, and thank you for being my sponsor and my friend.*

Sponsor: *I am glad to be your sponsor and friend. May you find the power you need to keep you on the right path.*

Then, if you are not shy about it, get on your feet and give each other a big hug. You will know that you have taken your First Step.

2

Second Step:
Came to believe that a power greater than ourselves could restore us to sanity.

WORK PLAN FOR STEP TWO

What to read and study. In ALCOHOLICS ANONYMOUS, read pages 44-57. In TWELVE STEPS AND TWELVE TRADITIONS, read pages 25-34. If you were into drugs, read pages 52-73 in NARCOTICS ANONYMOUS, and the text on Step Two, pages 22-24.

Meet with your sponsor. Share your doubts and fears about this step.

Exercise 1. Write about coming to believe:

1. As a child, what did you believe about a Supreme Being?
2. Were you turned off to God somewhere? How?
3. Did any other spiritual idea ever appeal to you? Describe it.
4. Write about where you are now in coming to believe.

Exercise 2. Write about a power greater than yourself.

1. Describe what a Higher Power is to you.
2. Describe times when a Higher Power came to your rescue.
3. Write a letter to your Higher Power.
4. Write a prayer in your own words to your Higher Power.

Exercise 3. Write about sanity issues. Describe five examples of your behavior while drinking and using that would hardly qualify as sanity.

Take the step with your sponsor. Read aloud everything you have written.

A closure to the Second Step. Find out if your sponsor has a wind-up for Step Two, and if it sounds good, use it. Or go together to a quiet place where you won't be disturbed. Try to overcome your self-consciousness, and kneel together. Say some prayers to make a little ceremony of taking the step. Sponsors may begin with a prayer in their own words, or may use a variation of the one below. Then, you read or speak the prayer you wrote in Exercise 2 above, or speak the one suggested below.

Sponsor: *Our Higher Power, we ask You to hear our words today as we kneel together in Your presence so that _____(name)_____ may formally take with You the Second Step of the program of recovery. Thank You for listening.*

Sponsee: *My Higher Power, today I acknowledge Your Presence and Your Power, and I welcome You into my life. I have come to believe that You, a power greater than myself, can restore me to sanity. Please do it for me now. Thank You for caring about me.*

Then both might say, singly or together:

Higher Power, give us Your grace, and let Your strength and power flow into us. May we receive them now.

Then get up off your knees and feel confident that you have taken the Second Step and have made a connection with your Higher Power.

3

Third Step:
Made a decision to turn our will and our lives over to the care of God as we understood Him.

WORK PLAN FOR STEP THREE

What to read and study. In ALCOHOLICS ANONYMOUS, study the text on Step Three, pages 60-63 In TWELVE STEPS AND TWELVE TRADITIONS, read pages 35-42. If you are addicted to drugs, in NARCOTICS ANONYMOUS read pages 74-89, and read Step Three, pages 24-26.

Meet with your sponsor. Discuss what you have read, and read out loud together some passages from these books. If this step scares you, talk frankly about it with your sponsor.

Exercise 1. Write about your obsession with yourself.

1. Give examples of when you were selfish and self-centered.
2. Describe ways in which your behavior was self-seeking.
3. Write about when and how you conned yourself.
4. Tell when and how you controlled and manipulated others.
5. Identify some of the hundred forms of fear that drove you.

Exercise 2. Write about God as you understand God.

1. Describe the God of your understanding.
2. List ten qualities of a God with whom you would feel safe.
3. Compose your own Third Step prayer to God. Write it out.

Take the step with your sponsor by sharing all you have written.

A closure to the Third Step. If your sponsor has a wrap-up for the step, do it. Or kneel with your sponsor and close with variations of these prayers. You say the prayer you wrote in Exercise

2. Or use the prayer below which Toby H. wrote for his Third Step.

> Sponsor: *God, we kneel together in Your presence so that* _____*(name)*_____ *may take with You the Third Step of the Twelve Step program of recovery. We pray that you will hear*_____(name's)_____words and receive this decision.

> Sponsee: *My Father, my Friend, my Creator, please take my hand, my life, and help me to understand that it is Your life that you have loaned to me. Please help me return it to You to do with as You will. Today, I make the decision to let go and let You, and to turn my will and my life over to Your care.*

Then say together the Third Step prayer from page 63 in the Big Book:

> *God, I offer myself to Thee—to build with me and to do with me as Thou wilt. Relieve me of the bondage of self, that I may better do Thy will. Take away my difficulties, that victory over them may bear witness to those I would help of Thy power, Thy love, and Thy way of life. May I do Thy will always!*

Then get up and go about your business. You have taken your Third Step.

4

Fourth Step:
Made a searching and fearless moral inventory of ourselves.

WORK PLAN FOR STEP FOUR

Before starting.work. Review your written work on Step Three.

What to read and study. In ALCOHOLICS ANONYMOUS, read pages 64-71. In TWELVE STEPS AND TWELVE TRADITIONS, read pages 43-55. If drugs were a problem, in NARCOTICS ANONYMOUS read pages 90-103, and read the text on Step Four, pages 27-30.

Exercise 1. Write about resentments. In one or two sentences, write about each resentment you hold, name the person or institution, tell why you are resentful, and tell what it does to you, for example:

> "I have a resentment against Debbie because she dumped me and moved in with John. This activates my fear of abandonment, hurts my self-esteem, and affects my sex life."

Exercise 2. Take action on resentments. Pray for the people you resent, using this prayer adapted from page 67 in the Big Book:

> *This is a sick person. God, help me to show the same tolerance, patience and pity that I would cheerfully grant a sick friend. How can I be helpful? God, save me from being angry. Thy will be done.*

Exercise 3. List your fears. Write about your fears, big ones and little ones, tell why you have each one, and how it impacts you, for example:

> "I have a fear of feeling inadequate, because my parents

told me I was dumb and would never amount to anything. I compensate by being defiant and arrogant."

Exercise 4. Write about your sex conduct. Write your own series of questions on your sex life, and how you selfishly used and abused your sex powers. Write out the answers. Use the examples below only as guides.

My relationship with_____(name) _____
What caused us to break up? Whom did I hurt?
Where was I to blame? In what ways was I selfish?
Where did I put myself first? Where did I lie?
Where was I thoughtless and uncaring?
Where was I irritable and unsympathetic?
How did I provoke jealousy? How should I have behaved?
Was I promiscuous in my sex life? How? When?
What sex hang-ups do I need to look at?
What is the major character defect?
What is the fear behind all this, if any?
What would be the ideal relationship for me?

Exercise 5. Action on sex conduct. We may want to pray for direction in making changes in our sexual behavior. These prayers are adapted from pages 69 and 70 in the Big Book:

God, I ask that you mold my ideals and help me to live up to them. Help me always to remember that my sex powers are God-given and therefore good, neither to be used lightly or selfishly nor to be despised and loathed.
God, I pray for the right ideal, for guidance in each questionable situation, and for the strength to do the right thing.

Exercise 6. Emotional/economic security. Make up a list of incidents where you have felt threatened, angry or insecure, and where you lied, stole or cheated. For example, an entry might read something like this:

"I feel insecure in my marriage. I am angry with my husband because he criticizes me constantly. I have lied to him and stolen money from him, and he knows it. He calls me a stupid drunk who can't be trusted. I am afraid to leave him."

Exercise 7. List your assets. Make a list of the good qualities which you know to be part of your character. If you are in doubt, ask relatives and friends whom you trust, and ask your sponsor for suggestions.

No closure to the Fourth Step. Consider your Fourth Step unfinished business until you have taken your Fifth Step. The closure for the Fourth Step is the Fifth Step itself. And the closure suggested in the Work Plan for Step Five is a wrap-up for both these steps.

5

Fifth Step:
Admitted to God, to ourselves, and to another human being the exact nature of our wrongs.

WORK PLAN FOR STEP FIVE

Before getting started. Make a decision on the person who is to hear your Fifth Step. Ask him or her now, and set a specific date.

What to read and study. In ALCOHOLICS ANONYMOUS, read pages 72-75. In TWELVE STEPS AND TWELVE TRADITIONS, read pages 56-63. In NARCOTICS ANONYMOUS read pages 30-32.

Exercise 1. Admitting to yourself. Start with a prayer. Invent your own, or use a variation of this one:

My Higher Power, be with me and help me to be completely honest in this talk I am about to have with myself. Please give me Your guidance and support.

Pull a comfortable chair close to a large mirror, and sit and look into your own eyes. Talk quietly to yourself, admitting your wrongs to your twin self in the mirror. Talk about your assets, then smile at your Spiritual Image in the mirror and watch that Image speak back to you as you say:

"I have heard your Fifth Step. I acknowledge it. And I forgive you for everything."

Exercise 2. Admitting to God. Some prefer to take this segment on their knees in a house of worship. If you are at home, move to a desk or table. Place a chair across from the one in which you sit. Close your eyes and try to visualize the presence of your God sitting in the chair opposite you. Begin speaking directly to your God, something like this:

My God, let me know You are near. Hear me now as I speak my Fifth Step of recovery and admit to You the exact nature of my wrongs. I tell You everything, so that there will be nothing hidden between us. Help me to be completely honest with You. Thank You, God, for listening.

When you have finished telling God the wrongs and defects, tell God about your good points. Then be silent for a while, reflecting on what you have done, and close with a prayer. Ask God, in your own words, to forgive you, or adapt this prayer:

My Creator, I ask Your forgiveness for the wrongs I have done. Help me to understand the character defects which lie behind these actions, and help me to clear up this wreckage, let go of it, and set things right where I can. Thank You, God.

Exercise 3. Admitting to another human being.

1. From brief notes, talk your Fifth Step—don't read it. Sit close to your listener, work up your courage, and just begin talking.
2. Don't be surprised if some strong emotions come out.
3. Don't rush it. Talk it all out.
4. Ask your listener to help you pinpoint your character defects.
5. Ask your listener to help you identify patterns of behavior.
6. When it is done, both people need to share their feelings about what was told. You should be prepared to accept suggestions and guidance.
7. Go home and spend an hour or so reflecting on what you have experienced. Mentally review the first five steps and question if there is anything you have omitted. Repeat this

prayer, adapted from the prayer at the conclusion of the Fifth Step in the Big Book, page 75:

God, I thank You from the bottom of my heart for letting me get to know You better.

A closure to the Fifth Step. Make, and guard, xerox copies of your inventory lists for reference in Steps Six through Nine. Then, if this idea appeals to you, go with your sponsor, take the original pages of your Fourth Step and find a place where it is safe to burn several pages of paper without danger of causing a fire. When you are ready, say something like this:

God, these are all happenings which belong to the past. These people and these events no longer have power over me. With Your help and Your forgiveness, I now consign them to the past and go forward to take the next steps in my recovery.

After praying, put a flame to each page, watch it burn, and watch the smoke drift away and disappear. Step on the ashes. In this ritual of fire, you celebrate the completion of your Fourth Step and your Fifth Step.

6

Sixth Step:
Were entirely ready to have God remove all these defects of character.

WORK PLAN FOR STEP SIX

Before starting work. Discuss your character defects with your sponsor. Select the three most glaring personality flaws and establish priorities, numbering them 1 through 3 in order of importance.

What to read and study. Read the paragraph on Step Six, top of page 76, in ALCOHOLICS ANONYMOUS. Read the personal story on pages 439-452. In TWELVE STEPS AND TWELVE TRADITIONS, read pages 64-70. If you were into drugs, read pages 33-34 in NARCOTICS ANONYMOUS.

Exercise 1. Write about three character defects. On each of your main character defects, ask yourself these questions and write out the answers.

Name of character defect: _____

1. In what way does this defect protect me?
2. How does it add to any negative pattern of behavior?
3. How would I be changed or different if I no longer had it?
4. How can I reprogram myself with a new attitude and action?

Exercise 2. Becoming entirely ready. Take one character defeat each ten days. Think about it daily. Each day, say the Sixth Step prayer, below, and insert the name of that particular character defect.

My God, I am now entirely ready to have You remove my

_____(name of defect) _____. *Help me to be willing to let go.*

At the end of ten days, move on to the next character defect and repeat the process. When thirty days are up, go on to the next three defects on your list.

Exercise 3. Write about cooperating with God. Write a short paragraph about what you intend to do to cooperate with God in the removal of each of your three principal character defects.

Take the step with your sponsor. Read aloud what you have written. Talk over your plans to cooperate with God in the removal of your first three defects.

A closure to the Sixth Step. Go with your sponsor to the quiet place where you capped the other steps. Kneel, originate your own prayers, or say these suggested ones, putting your name and your defects in the blank spaces:

> Sponsor: *God, once more we kneel together in Your presence,_____so that_____ (name)_____ may formally take the Sixth Step of the program of recovery. Hear our words, we pray.*

> Sponsee: *My God, I am now entirely ready to have You remove all my defects of character, especially: (here, speak the name of each of the three character defects.) Help me to cooperate with You in every way. Thank you, God.*

Then stand up, give each other a hug, and go on your way. You will have worked your Sixth Step to the best of your ability at this time.

7

Seventh Step:
Humbly asked Him to remove our shortcomings.

WORK PLAN FOR STEP SEVEN

Before getting started. Ask for your sponsor's input on working this step.

What to read and study. In ALCOHOLICS ANONYMOUS, read the second paragraph on page 76. Read the chapter on Step Seven in TWELVE STEPS AND TWELVE TRADITIONS, pages 71-78. Pay attention to the last paragraph, which contains the essence of the step. If you are addicted to drugs, in NARCOTICS ANONYMOUS read Step Seven, pages 34-36.

Exercise 1. Examine your attitudes on humility. In a dictionary, look up the definitions of *humble* and *humility*. Spend some time thinking deeply about how your attitudes have changed while working the first six steps. Ask yourself these questions, and write down your answers:

  1. How do I now understand the wider meaning of humility?
  2. How am I more humble now than I was before?
  3. How has a new perception of humility changed my outlook?

Exercise 2. Write a prayer. In your own words, compose a short prayer, and then say it daily. Ask God to teach you to be humble. Ask God to remove your shortcomings.

Exercise 3. Keep cooperating with God. Review the writing you did in Exercise 3 of Step Six about cooperating with God. Keep cooperating daily, practicing positive behaviors that help offset your negative shortcomings.

Take the step with your sponsor. Read aloud the prayer you wrote. Review together how your attitudes on humility may be changing. Talk over in detail how you are cooperating with God in the removal of your first three character defects. Discuss what you will do about the remaining ones.

A closure to the Seventh Step. Go to the quiet place and get on your knees with your sponsor. Close the step with prayers.

> Sponsor: *God, be with us for a while and listen as* ————— *(name)*————— *takes with You the Seventh Step of the program of recovery. Grant* ———————*(name's)* ————— *request, we pray. Thank You, Higher Power.*

At this point, say or read the prayer you composed in Exercise 2. Then go directly into the Seventh Step Prayer from page 76 in the Big Book.

SEVENTH STEP PRAYER

Sponsee: My Creator, I am now willing that You should have all of me, good and bad. I pray that You now remove from me every single defect of character which stands in the way of my usefulness to You and my fellows. Grant me strength, as I go out from here, to do Your bidding.

Then get up, honor each other with a hug, and leave with a good expectant feeling that your God has heard you and is going to work for you to release you from all your shortcomings.

8

Eighth Step:
Made a list of all persons we had harmed, and became willing to make amends to them all.

WORK PLAN FOR STEP EIGHT

What to read and study. In ALCOHOLICS ANONYMOUS, read pages 76-84. In TWELVE STEPS AND TWELVE TRADITIONS, read pages 79-84. If you abused other chemical substances, in NARCOTICS ANONYMOUS read pages 36-38.

Exercise 1. Complete your list. From your Fourth and Fifth Step notes, make up a list of names of people you harmed. Search your memory for any nearly-forgotten incidents and add these names to the list.

Exercise 2. Evaluate the harm. Check each name on your list against the following questions. If you score one or more Yes answers on any name, that name belongs on your list.

1. Did I lie to them?
2. Did I cheat them, or cheat on them?
3. Did I do them out of money or other material things?
4. Did my conduct make them seek revenge?
5. Was my behavior toward them irresponsible?
6. Did I behave selfishly?
7. Did I act distant and uncaring?
8. Was I emotionally stingy? Was I financially stingy?
9. Did I do things that gave them good cause to be jealous?
10. Did I wreck their calm and serenity?
11. Did I try to dominate them?
12. Did I try to tell them how to run their lives?
13. Did I often criticize them?
14. Was I frequently mean-tempered in dealing with them?
15. Did I frequently act impatient with them?

16. Did I often make them angry?
17. Did I openly neglect them when I should not have done so?

Exercise 3. Become willing. It is hard to become willing to make amends without first forgiving. Here is a simple prayer on willingness and forgiveness which you may repeat as often as you like.

> *My Higher Power, please help me to become willing to forgive the people I have harmed. Help me to become willing to make amends to them all.*

A forgiveness closure to the Eighth Step. Go with your sponsor to your secluded place. Sit for a few moments and meditate on forgiveness. Then kneel together, make up your own prayers of forgiveness, or say a variation of these:

> Sponsor: *God, be with us in this moment, and hear our words. Please help_____(name)_____to truly forgive and be willing to make amends to all persons who were harmed.*

> Sponsee: *My Higher Power, I am now willing to forgive, and willing to make amends to all persons whom I have harmed, especially: (then read all the names on your list.) Give me the strength to forgive and to make the amends I need to do.*

Then stand up, embrace, and decide if you like the following ceremony.

A forgiveness celebration. Buy a bunch of colored balloons inflated with helium gas, and get a black marker pen. Take the balloons to an open outdoor area and write on each balloon the first name of a person you harmed. Then, one by one, release each balloon as you say out loud the following affirmation:

_____(name)_____, *I now forgive you completely for everything that was between. us. I wish you all the best in your life. I release you and let you go. You are free, and I am free.*

Don't be surprised if you feel some strong emotions as you release each balloon and watch it take flight. There will be no question in your mind about whether or not you have done your Eighth Step. You will remember it.

9

Ninth Step:
Made direct amends to such people wherever possible, except when to do so would injure them or others.

WORK PLAN FOR STEP NINE

What to read and study. In ALCOHOLICS ANONYMOUS, read pages 76-84. In TWELVE STEPS AND TWELVE TRADITIONS, read pages 85-89. If drugs were a problem, in NARCOTICS ANONYMOUS read pages 39-40.

Before beginning. Review "Four-Part Amends Plan" in Chapter Nine.

Exercise 1. Establish priorities. Separate names on your list into three categories, and title them: 1) The No Problem List—people I can make amends to now; 2) The Maybe List—people I may or may not make amends to; 3) The No Way List—people I will probably never make amends to.

Exercise 2. Say the Ninth Step prayers from pages 79 and 83 in the Big Book before making any amends.

God, I am willing to go to any length to find a spiritual experience. I pray that You will give me strength and direction to do the right thing, no matter what the personal consequences may be. Show me the way of patience, kindness, tolerance and love.

Exercise 3. Write letters of amends to people on the No Problem List.

Exercise 4. Make your telephone calls. Follow up and speak directly with each person and ask for a date and time to see them within the next week.

Exercise 5. Meet them personally. Observe the suggestions in the "Four-Part Amends Plan." Take God into the meeting with you. Go in with your head up and look the person in the eye. Explain why you are there, admit your wrongs, apologize, ask forgiveness, and make reparation when you can.

Meet with your sponsor. After you make your first amends, give your sponsor a play-by-play description of what went on. Listen carefully to comments and advice that may help you in your next amends.

Exercise 6. Follow through. Go through the same process with persons on your Maybe List and your No Way list. It gets easier each time you do it.

A closure to the Ninth Step. When you have made several amends, and you are conscious of a feeling of relief and gratitude at the healing which takes place, then go alone, or with your sponsor, to your private place. Get down on your knees and give thanks to the God of your understanding. If you need help to get started, you might modify these words to fit your feelings:

My Higher Power, from the bottom of my heart I give thanks to You for the healing that is taking place in my life as I make amends to the people I have harmed. I am grateful for Your strength and direction in helping me to do the right thing. Thank You for Your presence and Your power in my life.

Bear in mind that there is actually no real closure to Step Nine. The Big Book says it is a process which may very well continue for a lifetime.

10

Tenth Step:
Continued to take personal inventory and when we were wrong promptly admitted it.

WORK PLAN FOR STEP TEN

What to read and study. Read pages 84-85 in ALCOHOLICS ANONYMOUS. In TWELVE STEPS AND TWELVE TRADITIONS, read pages 90-97. You might read pages 41-42 in NARCOTICS ANONYMOUS.

Exercise 1. Practice the quick inventory. On small cards, write the words "radar sweep inventory." Tape these reminders on your mirror, dashboard, or at your desk or work station. Spot-check situations all during your day.

Exercise 2. Start daily inventorying. At bedtime, run a mental videotape of the day gone by. When something didn't go right, make a note on a small pad. Next day, admit you were wrong and correct it.

Exercise 3. Write a Focused Tenth Step inventory. Review Chapter Ten. Take any situation in your life which may be bothering you. Write out some questions. Talk with your Inner Guide and with your sponsor. Then write out the answers that come to you. Try these questions on a relationship problem:

> What am I not getting from this relationship?
> What do I really need in this relationship?
> Are my wants and needs selfish, self-centered?
> Will I get my needs met in this relationship?
> What are the problems in this relationship?
> Am I willing to work at solving those problems?
> Is the other person willing to work at it also?
> Are we both willing to seek counseling on it?

166

Do I really want to continue in the relationship?
Would I be afraid to live alone?
Would I be relieved if it were over?
Do I really want out?
Do I have the guts to try to resolve it?
Am I manipulating the other into terminating it?
What is my main character defect operating here?
What are my options?
What action shall I take?

Take the step with your sponsor. Discuss your progress in daily inventorying. Read aloud your written Tenth Step. Get your sponsor to help spot your character defects and the options and actions you should consider.

A closure to the Tenth Step. Go with your sponsor to your serene place. Kneel, and say this prayer adapted from Step Ten in the Twelve and Twelve.

Thank You, God, for the blessings I have received from You. Help me to do to others as I would have them do to me.

If you have done the work, you will have learned daily inventorying, done your written Tenth Step, and learned the problem-solving process.

11

Eleventh Step:
Sought through prayer and mediation to improve our conscious contact with God *as we understood Him,* **praying only for knowledge of His will for us and the power to carry that out.**

WORK PLAN FOR STEP ELEVEN

What to read and study. In ALCOHOLICS ANONYMOUS, read pages 85-88. In TWELVE STEPS AND TWELVE TRADITIONS, read pages 98-108. If you did drugs, in NARCOTICS ANONYMOUS read pages 43-47.

Exercise 1. Conscious contact through prayer. Put together your own prayer program for working Step Eleven. Compose basic prayers—at first, write them out, then change them around a little each time you say them.
1. Make up a brief prayer for talking with God each morning.
2. Work out a prayer for talking with God at bedtime.
3. Create a "Help!" prayer for when you're in trouble.
4. Build a prayer of thanks and gratitude.
5. Develop a quick "Just touching bases" prayer.
6. Do a prayer asking for knowledge of God's will for you.
7. Invent a prayer asking for power to carry out a God-plan or idea, saying you claim the power and accept responsibility for it.

Exercise 2. Conscious contact through meditation. Plan ahead a special prayer and meditation session when you will be alone, without interruptions, and have plenty of time. First, read a beautiful spiritual passage and meditate on its beauty. Kneel or sit comfortably. Say a prayer, then contemplate how deeply you would like to make intimate contact with God. After a while, say in your heart something like *I seek the One known as God the*

Father or *I seek the God of my understanding.* Quietly wait to see if you may experience an awareness of God's energy and presence flowing into you.

Exercise 3. God's plan for you. Meditate at length on what God's plan for you might be. Allow the God-Head in you to roam anywhere and imagine anything. Afterward, write down the thoughts that came to you.

Exercise 4. Signposts of empowerment.

1. Think, then write about an incident when you clicked with God's power inside you and were able to do something you thought you couldn't do.
2. Write three examples of present situations in which you know that God's power is in you, operating now in your life.

Exercise 5. Practice meditating. Set aside twenty minutes either in the morning or the evening and try to make a habit of daily meditation. If you can afford it, consider taking a course in meditation.

Take the step with your sponsor. Read aloud all you have written. Share your experience in your meditation seeking conscious contact with God.

A closure to the Eleventh Step. Go to your usual place with your sponsor and do a prayer and a joint meditation together. Kneel and pray:

God, I am seeking through prayer and meditation to improve my conscious contact with You. Thank You for revealing Your Presence to me. Grant me, each day, knowledge of Your will for me and the power to carry that out.

Taking down the wall. Do a creative imagery meditation with your sponsor. Sit side by side, get comfortable, close your eyes, and meditate together for about twenty minutes, each on this theme:

> In your mind's eye, picture the wall containing the door that was separating you from God, the door mentioned in Step Three. Focus your power through the center of your forehead, beam it at the wall, and visualize the wall cracking all over, splitting, coming apart, slowly crumbling and falling down in a line of rubble. As the dust settles, you step over the debris that once was the wall, and you see you are in another place. Imagine that you are embraced by Someone on the other side. Who is it?

12

Twelfth Step:
Having had a spiritual awakening as the result of these steps, we tried to carry this message to alcoholics and addicts and to practice these principles in all our affairs.

WORK PLAN FOR STEP TWELVE

What to read and study. Read pages 89-103 in ALCOHOLICS ANONYMOUS. In TWELVE STEPS AND TWELVE TRADITIONS, read pages 109-130. If narcotics were a factor, read pages 48-51 in NARCOTICS ANONYMOUS.

Before getting started. Discuss with your sponsor the state of your spiritual awakening. Then ask for advice on working with others in your groups.

Exercise 1. Your spiritual awakening. Meditate on what has happened in your spiritual development. Let your thoughts drift back in time to events which may actually have been spiritual experiences, even though you didn't recognize them as such at the time. In your notebook or journal, write and describe in detail your first awareness of your spiritual awakening.

Exercise 2. Working with others. Find out what outreach service work your group is doing. Volunteer and sign up. Make an outline plan of action, set some deadlines, and do it. Make up a prayer—Tell God you need someone to sponsor, to help the newcomer and to help you. Ask God to send someone to you, then look around for somebody to appear.

Exercise 3. Practice these principles. For a month or more, to encourage it as a habit, carry in your shirt pocket or purse a small wire-bound notebook. Be alert to sense times when you are actually practicing a program principle in your affairs to better a situation. Recognize it and record it.

Take the step with your sponsor. Tell what you do to work with others. Give examples of where you worked the principles and what happened.

A closure to the Twelfth Step. Step Twelve is meant to be an ongoing process in our lives. However, we may acknowledge our working of the step by going with our sponsor to the special place, kneeling together, saying a prayer of gratitude and a request for guidance.

> *God, thank You for Your presence and Your power within me. I am grateful to You for bringing me through the Twelve Steps of recovery and showing me this new way of life. Help me to know the joy of working with others, and help me to practice these principles in all my affairs, now and in the future.*

Congratulate yourself for becoming a sober, responsible, caring person, and for sticking with the Twelve Step program. Then embrace your sponsor and say something along these lines:

> *Thank you for being my sponsor. Thank you for being my good friend and for caring about me. I am grateful for your patience and your guidance. The wisdom you shared with me is now part of my experience. May God bless you and keep you.*